VILLAGE ␣ .

Uplifting Communities the Maher Way

Darcy Cunningham

To Donate to Maher: maherashram.org

Or

USgivingtomaher.org

I offer this book in love and tribute to Maher, her people, her works.

May all who read it be also uplifted.

Contents

FOREWORD

Happy Welcome! When we opened our first small home in 1997, Maher's intention was to provide care and shelter for women fleeing domestic violence along with the children they brought with them. At that time, I had no idea that Maher, which means "Mother's Home" in Marathi, would one day grow to more than 68 residential homes and 25 outreach programs in seven Indian states.

I am deeply grateful to long-time volunteer and US Giving to Maher Board Chair Darcy Cunningham for coming forward to tell the important story of the work we do *outside* of our homes. You will learn, as we did, the power local social work efforts have to change lives and society.

Maher's mission is to help the destitute in India exercise their right to a higher quality of life, irrespective of gender, caste, creed, or religion. Three unshakeable pillars of our service to humanity and nature are gender equality, justice, and interfaith harmony. In a country rich with faith traditions, we decided early on that at Maher "love is our religion." While we have witnessed countless miracles in people's lives when they feel safe, a part of the Maher family and loved, it is our dream that one day there will be no need for shelter homes like ours.

Earlier books have told the story of the significant obstacles we faced as we worked to create caste-free, interfaith spaces where we could walk toward wholeness with destitute, abandoned women, children, and later men. This book delves more deeply into what we came to understand is needed for the people and communities we serve to break free from violence, poverty, and oppression in empowering and sustainable ways.

Today, India is home to more than 1.4 billion people. As much as Maher has grown, we can serve only a tiny fraction of those in need in our four walls. We can, as Darcy will show you in these pages, open our loving and supportive arms to many more through community-based efforts. It brings us great joy to open preschools in the slums, to offer relief when disasters strike, to present street plays on health education topics and violence prevention, and to sponsor more than 700 self-help groups in 90 villages.

Maher's work would not be possible without the unwavering commitment of our staff and our volunteers and supporters in India and around the globe. Most importantly, we owe our deepest gratitude to the women, children, and men it is our blessing to serve. Their strength and resolve shine like beacons of hope for one another, their families, neighbors, the people of India, the world, and all of us.

At Maher, one of our favorite songs is "We Are the World." "We are the ones who make a brighter day, so let's start giving." I hope what we have learned helps you in your service.

At Maher, one of our core values is that "there is always room for one more." Please know you are always welcome at Maher.

Lead with love,

Sr. Lucy Kurien
Founder -Director Maher

INTRODUCTION

WHY THIS BOOK? TERRITORY IT COVERS

Maher (Mother's Home) has become widely known both in India and in the West for its wonderful work helping destitute women, children, families, mentally disturbed women and men, and more. There have been several books published in the U.S. documenting the work and stories of some of Maher's people. However little has been written about Maher's extensive work and programs out in the slums, villages and tribal areas. Maher has expanded significantly, both within the state of Maharashtra as well as to six more states in India, yet managed to maintain its core values. Walk into any Maher center and you know you are at Maher! This too has never been written about. The current volume fills these gaps.

PREVIOUS BOOKS ABOUT MAHER

Women Healing Women by Will Keepin and Cynthia Brix was the first. This volume showcases one of Maher's unique methods of healing. Housemothers and many of Maher's social workers first came to Maher destitute themselves. Women (and children) who come to Maher seeking help receive support, education, healing, skills, and whatever they need to live an independent life. As they heal, these women become housemothers assisting with the care of children mostly, but also other residents. Serving as staff supports their healing and they have experience and empathy to

1

support the next to arrive, plus they earn an income. Many stay on, remaining as housemothers while others train to become social workers.

Dignity From Despair: A Step By Step Guide For Transforming the Lives of Women and Children – Successful NGO Creation Using the Maher Model by Darcy Cunningham describes in detail how to replicate Maher in other parts of India, and is applicable also in Africa, indeed anywhere. This book covers the territory from visioning the project, narrowing to a workable focus, selecting a site, operating values and procedures, hiring and training staff, sample work flows for incoming residents, and more.

Rising to New Life: Stories from Maher by Darcy Cunningham shares many stories of the women, children, even men, who have come through Maher's doors during their first 25 years of operation. This book also has a chapter on Maher's founder, Sister Lucy Kurien, sharing insight into how her life experiences shaped her, and how she thinks and problem solves in Maher's daily life.

These works detail a great deal about Maher's first two primary projects: women and children. The next few projects, such as Homes for mentally disturbed and mentally/physically challenged from birth, and a few others are also covered.

EXPANDING THE MISSION: BEYOND SHELTER HOMES

Sister Lucy soon realized that relying on shelters significantly limited how many people Maher could help. Maher's vision has always been to create an India where all her people thrive and there is no need for shelters such as Maher. Therefore, very early on, Maher began taking the work out into the villages, slums and tribal areas of India. While visitors to Maher get to see this work first-hand, nothing has been formally documented.

True to form, Maher's work centers on building trust and long-term relationships, family by family, village by village. Innovative programs developed in small incremental steps lead to lasting results. All of Sister Lucy's work is based on looking out to the people, listening, noticing patterns, and creatively working to address underlying root issues of poverty, violence, illiteracy, isolation and despair.

Spreading values

From Maher's beginning Sister Lucy, following her heart and her conscience, worked according to several strong beliefs and values, guided by her heart yet firmly interfaith. These values still guide Maher today. For Maher to realize her vision that all the people of India thrive and live to their potential, then families and villages must also thrive and all members must be free to live their potential - regardless of caste, religion, gender, wealth, etc.

These values led directly to promoting many new cultural norms, for example: educating girl-children, allowing widows

3

to remarry, respecting all faiths/religions, social justice for all people and castes, updated hygiene and sanitation, tending to the biosphere and climate change, and much more.

"Be the change you want to see in the world"

These are massive goals and challenges in India. Maher has had amazing successes and learned much along the way. How and what Maher has accomplished beyond its gates is the focus of this volume.

This book will bring light to these programs in villages, slums and tribal areas in the hope that these parts of Maher's work can also be replicated, in India and elsewhere. Maher has also extended its work to such neglected communities such as brick kiln workers, sugar cane migrant workers, and the needs of their families.

Maher has grown from its first center in a village outside Pune, to centers in seven states across India. You will read three examples how this growth has proceeded, and the challenges and lessons learned along the way that affect all future growth.

Finally, Maher's experience has led to some creative responses to large disasters, such as a major cyclone affecting Kolkata and the lockdowns and multiple challenges and misery of COVID-19.

BRIEF REMINDER OF MAHER'S CORE PROJECTS

Matruchaya

Homes for destitute, battered, physically challenged, and old-age women. (Maher's website describes the many programs that serve women.)

The word "Matruchaya" refers to the loving shadow cast by mothers toward their children. Women come to Maher from difficult life situations, many have faced violence, and suffer physical, emotional, psychological, social, and financial challenges. They come as mothers, widows, elderly, destitute, mentally challenged, unwanted pregnant women/girls, and more. Maher welcomes them and supports them in every possible way to help them rise to new life.

Some of the women, once healed, have completed a basic education, some go on to train for roles as nurses, teachers, social workers and more. Some remain at Maher in these roles, others return to their villages to work there and re-establish nurturing homes for their families.

Maher has housed more than 4637 women in its first 26 years, some for months, years, or even the rest of their life.

Kishoredham

Embracing orphans, children from broken or poverty-stricken families.

The name "Kishoredham" implies the joy and happiness that Maher believes is the basic right of every child. Maher works toward the well-being and education of every child who joins the Maher family. Children come to Maher due to poverty, trauma, or abandonment and are missing many of the requirements for healthy development and growth. Many the children come with their mothers but even they have, at the least, lost out on the chance for a secure home and education, and all too often also carry painful burdens from their past. Maher intentionally creates an atmosphere of love, acceptance and stability that is supportive of the emotional and physical growth of all children, enabling them to realize their full potential.

Maher has housed and educated over 4237 children; currently they are housing approximately 895 children. No matter the age they arrive, they are supported through a full education, including University, as per their interests and abilities. Currently more than 90 are pursuing higher education in various fields. Others receive vocational skills or professional training, such as nurses, police, chefs, teachers, tailors, and more.

At Maher's beginning, most women who came brought their children. All were housed in one communal space. However, Sister Lucy soon realized that a larger number of smaller Homes, each with fewer children, would provide more "home-like" living and better support the individual emotional needs of the children. Now each Children's Home houses 20-25 children each with two housemothers to care for them, preparing meals, washing clothing, helping with schoolwork, tucking them in at night, just as in a family home. There is a trained social worker for every group of three homes to monitor and support the progress and well-being of each home. These small Homes are another unique feature of Maher.

Pitruchaya

Homes for destitute, battered, physically challenged, and old age men.

The word "Pitruchaya" means "shadow of father." Over the years Sister Lucy would see destitute men on the streets, many injured, ill, often elderly, generally abandoned. Indian law prohibited her from housing men on the same premises as women or children, so she had never been able to help them.

One day, in 2011, Lucy learned of a man lying on the streets in very bad condition: strong body odor, badly torn clothes, dirty hair and sores on his body. She sent a social worker and several of the older boys to pick him up from the street. They brought him back to Maher to the older boys' Home, cleaned him up and got him medical attention and helped this man heal. This was the initiation of Pitruchaya project and Maher's Trustees agreed to expand Maher's mission. A few others were helped too, but because she could not keep men on the same premises as women (even though a different building), she had to stop this and wait until there could be a totally separate building and grounds for men.

In about two years, Lucy noticed an abandoned gas station near another large Maher facility. She convinced the owner to rent it to Maher for the men. Maher renovated the building, adding windows, doors, bathrooms, a kitchen and sleeping areas. Maher could again help these destitute, ill, often elderly, men. Here too, some of the men stayed on as housefathers to help in the care of the men, while others were healed and rehabilitated with their families, and the elderly could die with dignity when it was their time.

You can read more about all three of these projects in the above-mentioned books about Maher.

Sources

Sister Lucy was a major source of information for this volume. This author has visited Maher multiple times over the last 13 years, gathering stories and information as well as simply observing Maher's people at work. During COVID a group of us in the U.S. began hosting regular ZOOMs with Sister Lucy so we could follow her amazing work in those difficult times. These sessions also provided lots of stories and data.

Sister Lucy could not have accomplished all she has without the amazing, dedicated staff of Maher. The women who came seeking shelter and healing and who stayed as housemothers to support the next women and children to arrive. The social workers from the cities who wanted to work more directly with the people, to have maximum impact. The nuns, cousins and friends, who saw Sister Lucy's work and wanted to join her. This author has come to know many of them. There are too many to name them all, but some of these stories were impossible to tell without naming a few. Hirabegum Mulla (Hira to all) and Anand Sagar were the first two social workers Lucy hired about one year after beginning Maher. Both are still with Maher. Hira speaks English and so was a major source of information for this volume. Several other senior social workers, staff and residents, whom this author has known since my first visit, have been practicing English over the years with foreign guests. They were sources for some of the special stories, so you will hear their names too.

Many Indian people and companies have helped Maher over the years, including donations of buildings or land, or land at below-market costs. Again, these are too many to name, and none of the individual donors are listed by name. Their support nonetheless has been critical and is deeply appreciated.

Finally, Maher's website is continually being updated with photos and information as is their FaceBook page and Instagram. Links are available in the Appendix.

Note: names of Maher residents and beneficiaries have been changed to protect their privacy.

1: BEYOND SHELTER HOMES
A Patchwork Quilt of Services

WHY THE NEED TO EXPAND?

A year after opening its doors, Maher was literally over-flowing with women and children. Sister Lucy quickly realized she could not bring every woman and child to Maher, let alone help all the families in need. She saw people living in the dirt (literally), parents rag-picking along the roadside for 12-15 hours a day in hopes of earning a bit of food to eat; she found children being trained to beg. She witnessed how the poor, who were also illiterate, were taken advantage of and so often cheated, even if they could find work or buy food. She saw loving parents doing their best to care for their children, but unable to provide regular food, medical care, education, even the basics. Sister Lucy always believed the ideal for children is to be raised in a loving family home, rather than an institution, even one as wonderful as Maher.

Sister Lucy is an amazing listener. Not only does she focus on the person in front of her, she also listens between the lines. She hears what the woman isn't saying, as well as the words spoken. And then Sister Lucy connects the dots; she instinctively looks for root causes and underlying conditions and factors. It was this capacity to listen to the women she took in, and to their families discuss their difficulties, which sent her out to the villages and slums. There she talked to the people and listened more.

Sister Lucy quickly came to understand that poverty is a central underlayer to the violence and other challenges she witnessed in families. The "chain" she saw was that poverty led to a lack of food and housing security, which contributed to ill health, lack of education, despair, which in turn contribute to alcoholism, abuse and violence. These reinforce the lack of a way out, further deepening despair. She saw illiterate adults and a lack of education for children, especially girl-children. It is a cycle with seemingly no end. She also saw caste, gender, religious prejudices and superstitions hindering villagers from working together.

She knew she had to find a way to support families where they lived to rise above stark poverty and to be able to raise their children with love and basic needs being met, including education. They would need to do more for children in their homes, families, villages and even in the slums and beggars' colonies. She also came to firmly believe that education offered a key to ending the cycle, especially for the next generation.

Maher's ultimate vision became clear: an India where there is no longer a need for Maher; women and families are healthy and safe; no children end up on the streets; all children are safe, loved, educated and have the possibility to dream and achieve their dreams.

HOW: WE SEE HOW IT IS AND WE DO THE NEEDFUL

Toward this vision, Sister Lucy and early staff began to create solutions to stabilize and strengthen the families at home. These became known at Maher as a Patchwork Quilt of Services. Each program was born in response to needs seen and responded to.

"We see how it is." And then we "Do the needful" are two phrases every visitor to Maher has heard over and over. This practice led to the creation of each one of the programs below.

Sister Lucy began in simple small steps: a solution for one family became a program that other families could tap into. For example, Maher delivered a monthly allotment of food staples (rice, lentils, oil, flour) to poor families; staff started teaching about general nutrition and hygiene; blankets were distributed; kindergartens (including food) were begun, wells were dug. And more, according to the needs of the local people.

In this process, Sister Lucy, Maher, and her social workers became well-known, liked and trusted in the surrounding villages. Maher never went anywhere and told people what they must do. Instead, Maher helped solve problems as identified by the villagers, or brought food, clothing and blankets. Sister Lucy listened to the people as they begin to talk about their troubles. Medical care was made available when someone was gravely ill, and invitations to programs extended. Relationships were developed.

In this way, fairly quickly, a whole host of programs arose to stabilize families, villages, even in slums, so all could *rise to new life*. Far, far more people and families are supported than those who actually live in a Maher Home. These programs spread to every new site Maher develops; when a new Home in a new region or state is opened, many more people are helped than just those in the shelter homes.

12

WHAT AROSE FROM DOING THE NEEDFUL

"Stabilize a village and you have stabilized many families."

It's a process: there was not a sequential pre-planned rolling out of programs. Each program arose to meet a need in the moment. As it was implemented, it was refined, developed and its use spread. Below are descriptions of many of these programs, sometimes with anecdotal stories demonstrating the effect beyond a single individual.[1]

Pragati (Awareness Raising)

Pragati means progress. Awareness Raising is a key program and while it started with the basics such as hygiene and dangers of alcoholism and superstitions, difficult topics such as domestic violence and ending the caste system were soon included.

One early lesson Maher learned was the need for a lot of awareness-raising and education in the villages about basic things like hygiene, the value of education, dangers of alcoholism, addressing superstitions, and more. They realized they needed the support of, and good relationships with, the local villages or these people would sabotage Maher.

---

[1] A full list of programs is included in Appendix 2. As of 2021 at least 136,235 people were reached through these programs. (Source June 2021 Maher zoom talk) With the recent addition since 2021 of several new Maher centers, this number will grow very quickly.

For example: Maher's first building had modern indoor Indian toilets. This is a porcelain squatting platform, with a flush pull-cord and a water spigot for washing up. The villagers held old beliefs held that it was dangerous to "go inside;" the villagers used the streets and fields and there was excrement everywhere. When they heard Maher had "inside toilets" they stormed the place and destroyed the new modern indoor toilets believing they were "unhygienic," even evil!

The people in the villages were mostly illiterate, so Maher could not hand out flyers or post signs. Maher began creating and performing short entertaining street plays on various topics. These plays became the main medium to get the messages out to the villagers to help them understand new ideas and healthy practices.

Maher staff and residents would walk the village inviting all to come, sometimes also playing music, then do a small play on the chosen theme. Village people would gather to watch. Often nearly the whole village would gather around: men, women, children. Some would come talk to Maher people afterwards, and they also discussed these plays among themselves. This is one way Maher began to become known in a village and to develop relationships and trust.

At first the women and staff created and performed these plays; in later years the older "college-going"[2] children wrote and performed the plays. These youth are the future for the

---

[2] The phrase "college-going children" is used at Maher to refer to young people attending post-secondary education, and is used liberally in this book. Other common English phrases heard at Maher are also used in this book, though they sound unusual to western English speakers, such as "doing the needful."

villages. It is wonderful when young people can go back to the village they came from and bring the messages of interfaith, unity, stopping violence in the families, educate the girl-children, etc. These young people literally bring the future back to the villages.

Sometimes a talk or more in-depth program followed the street play. Music and dance performances were also used to gather the people where they were then invited to a longer program. Then Maher staff (or an expert such as a doctor) would give a short program. Other times, Maher sent word that a program would be happening and everyone who attended would receive a warm meal and a blanket. This attracted the people to come and to stay through the program. Staff tried to present the information as interestingly as possible. Of course not all truly paid heed, but slowly over time, relationships were built, eyes and minds were opened, and habits changed. This is part of "building trust" and is still the foundation of Maher's work with any village.

Cultural issues are tackled through these Awareness-Raising sessions too - such as educating girl-children, interfaith and the need to respect all religions, allowing widows to re-marry, domestic violence, socio-economic and gender-based justice, lessons of Gandhi, the caste system, and more.

Each year Maher conducts many awareness programs in villages near all their centers to educate, inform, change attitudes and improve the lives of villagers. These programs have spread also to interior and tribal villages, significantly contributing to improved life for all.

A partial list of topics:

- Health, hygiene and general wellbeing
- Dangers of alcoholism
- Value of education
- Safe pregnancy
- New mother and child healthcare
- Legal awareness and aid (especially for women)
- Human rights
- Superstitions
- Dowry system
- Child labor
- Female feticide
- Educating girl-children
- Domestic violence
- Sex education
- Inter-caste unity
- Interfaith, tolerance and respect for all religions
- Village hygiene and caring for the earth (ecology)
- Occupational opportunities

This author has attended several street plays when visiting Maher. One was about the dangers of alcohol, as many of the men in the village drank too much and were violent in the families when drunk. Maher's college-going young people and a few housemothers acted out scenes from a typical family life. A quiet family dinner became a scene of violence to the women and children when the father/husband came in drunk and started yelling and hitting. They showed the fear in the children, the harm to the mother, the shame in front of neighbors. Most of this was acted out, with little talking, and even I could understand without speaking the language. The whole village seemed to be watching, including many adult men. I wondered what they thought as they watched. They did not walk away or heckle; they were respectful even if quiet. Perhaps they could see themselves in new light and began to make new choices over time. Additionally, Maher social workers were there to support them with counseling, skill training and job placement.

Another time the offering was a longer program about the value of education, including for girl-children.[3] "Advertising" for this program was mostly word of mouth via the social workers and the local self-help groups. Attendees were promised a warm meal and a blanket for attending. There was a spacious community room ready and Maher staff went early to start cooking. This author was there with other white western guests. For villagers, seeing white people was another part of the attraction! The program was well-attended; some of the residents were familiar with Maher, some even knew some of the staff. They introduced their neighbors. Maher's social workers mingled and spoke with the people. Some of the people asked Maher for books for a library, others asked for a well. Plans for a next visit and more

---

[3] In India families often do not bother to educate the girls since they go to live with their in-laws once married. *"Educating a daughter is like watering the neighbor's garden"* is a common saying.

programs were begun. Like this, slowly, slowly relationships are built and even more can be done.

As Maher grew, another tool they have used is organizing marches and rallies on issues such as rape when a well-publicized national case came up, or it happened locally. Other marches have been in honor of International Women's Day, environmental and climate change awareness and value of Interfaith. These events draw people from multiple villages and along the roads marched, as well as bring press coverage.

For the International Women's Day 2020 march in Vadhu, 100's of people joined: women, men, children. You can see Sister Lucy leading the march.

Sister Lucy leading a march against violence towards women after a young woman was raped in India.

Ekta - food provisions and more

Ekta implies unity and togetherness. When a few parents asked Maher to admit their children saying that they were unable to provide them food, Maher realized that if they could provide food rations, then most of these families could remain living together. This project arose to provide rations like rice, wheat, oil, soya beans, etc., once a month or as per the need to those families who are under the poverty line, with the intention of keeping the family united and together despite the poverty. The regular provisions provide a sense of security to the family.

Often, helping a family in this way made the difference so children could go to school instead of working. When Maher staff found children on the streets begging or working menial jobs, staff inquired why they weren't in school. They asked to meet their families. Usually, poverty was the issue and the children were helping support the family to keep them all from starving. For example, Gamal at age seven was washing cars during the day and washing dishes out behind a restaurant in the evenings. His father was injured, could no longer work, and his mother was also working two jobs. They were barely surviving. So when Maher offered them the chance for Gamal to go to school (while living at Maher all expenses paid), they also promised to provide food supplies to the family so they would not starve without his income. Maher later helped with medical care for the mother. Now Gamal, 20+ years later is grown up, well-educated, working, married, and is supporting his mother and the last sister still unmarried. The whole family has *risen to new life*.

Sometimes bad health is the reason a family does not have enough money to buy food. Major operations or terminal illness make the medical expenses very high, which the poor cannot afford. When possible, Maher extends these people some or all of the costs. (There is no government-provided health care for anyone in India.)

Rachel's story - Three generations helped!
This story was told by Sister Lucy.

"Rachel became a widow when her husband had a stroke and died. She was left alone with one son and no way to earn money to help support him. They were very poor and had no other family to help them.

"She learned about Maher and approached me asking for help. She owned the home from her husband and was otherwise able to care for her home and son. Instead of bringing her and her son into Maher (which would also cause them to lose their home), we decided it is better to let them live in their house and support them there. With the simple provision of food, the family could remain together, living in their own home. This is also cheaper for Maher and allows our resources to spread to help more people.

"Then this son contracted and survived polio, though his left hand was deformed. It was hard to find a wife for him due to this and their poverty. As he got older, Rachel worried he would never marry. Again she approached me for assistance finding a wife. They were a good family, just poor.

"Meanwhile, Bhavani was found on the streets. The police brought her to us. She was mentally disturbed when she arrived. She was several months pregnant. She was weak, her legs all swollen. She was in very bad shape. We helped her to get healthier. We took her to hospital for the delivery and she was able to deliver the baby safely. She chose to give the baby for adoption. She regained her health mostly and left Maher. We do not know whether she went mad while on the streets, or was put out because she had troubles, nor do we know if she was raped or how she got pregnant again. We do not know her history.

"We got her healthy again – physically and mentally – not 100% but ok. She was living and working at Maher. She began to ask for us to get her married. She wanted to be in a family.

"She was able to tell us where her family lived. Staff took her there to see if they would take her back. They said go, put her back on the streets. We do not want her. So we brought her back with us to Maher."

How to find a good man and family for her?

"So when Rachel came looking for a wife for her son, I thought of Bhavani. They were about the right ages for each other. We let them meet and they liked each other. (Maher always tells both parties all the truth about each other, so nothing is secret. They must come to accept each other as they are.) Bhavani went for holiday a couple of times to stay with Rachel, her son, and Rachel's sister-in-law who also lived with them. They got along well, and both wanted to marry. So Maher got them married. They had two boys.

"Then Bhavani's husband (Rachel's son) died suddenly. The two boys were still small. By this time the sister-in-law was bed-ridden, Rachel was too old to work, and Bhavani was also unable to work outside due to her mental condition, though she could manage the children and the household ok.

22

"Maher stepped in with provisions of grain and food staples. This way with only the food provisions for assistance the whole family is able to live independently in their own home. Otherwise they would have ended up on the street. This is best for the family's dignity and long-term well-being and cheaper for Maher. Otherwise, Maher would have had to take in five people! Recently the two children had received free admission to a good Catholic boarding school."

Author's note: food provisions were part of this "solution" at different times, but other programs (such as support for unwed mothers) were interwoven. This is a good example of Maher doing the needful, but also of how the different programs of the Patchwork Quilt can work together.

Lokmangala – Public welfare in times of emergency

Lokmangala means community or public welfare. This project was started to address urgent and immediate needs in times of crisis and to provide relief during any natural calamity such as a flood, earthquake, tsunami or any man-made calamity or pandemic. The immediate objective is to give support during times of uncertainty. Wherever there is a Maher presence, staff is aware and prepared to jump into action.

One example was the flood impacting the slum of Miraj where Maher had taken over a small Home. This flood was unexpected and swift, quickly overwhelming people, especially those nearest the river. Staff immediately started distribution of ready-to-eat food. Later they provided dry food grain kits, tarpaulins and blankets. As the need arose, staff responded. See Chapter 6 for more examples of this project in response large, far-reaching disasters such as COVID, where upwards of 60,000 were helped in just one year, or the Great Cyclone of 2020 affecting Kolkata.

There are also individual families who approach Maher for assistance in times of sickness, needs for repair and renovation of their homes, support for academic progress of their children, or construction of toilets or water scarcity. Maher does its best to reach as many needy people as it can. At first, in a given year, more than 100 people/families were helped. These numbers have grown, and at least 6589 individuals/families were helped by the end of 2020.

One early example of Lokmangala for a single family as told to this author.

Sweta lived in Kendur village with her parents and younger brother. She was deaf since birth. When Sweta was about four years old, her parents took her to K.E.M. Hospital in Pune. After a couple of tests, the doctors told her parents that she needed to have surgery and she would be able to hear. They said the total cost would be Rs. 7,50, 000 rupees [about $10,200 USD] including medicines.

This amount was far beyond what Sweta's parents could afford. Her father ran a small snack center in Kendur village and earned a meager amount. Her mother was mostly ill and unable to work, plus the family had two very young children to care for. Her father was the sole support of the family.

Sweta's father had approached many people for help. He sent letters to companies in Pune, requesting financial aid for her surgery. After being turned down by many, TATA company came forward and donated Rs 3,00,000 rupees to them, about half the total cost. Sweta's father was able to collect another Rs. 1, 94, 000 rupees from friends and family. K.E.M. Hospital further helped them with Rs. 60,000 rupees. Even with all this, they were still short by Rs. 1, 96, 000 rupees so the doctors were unwilling to do the surgery.

The family did not know where else to go. Then one of the doctors brought Sweta and her parents to Maher. They met with Sister Lucy and Maher agreed to help Sweta. Maher sent emails to their contacts and was able to raise Rs 2,00,000 rupees – enough for Sweta's surgery.

The doctors operated and the surgery was successful. Post-surgery, one of Maher's social workers made regular visits to Sweta's family to supervise her recovery.

Eight years later, Sweta was twelve years old and studying in the sixth standard. She was a very happy child and on the way to normalcy. Her parents were overjoyed and deeply grateful to Maher for the assistance provided.

Swachata: Environmental and Hygiene Programs

India has a HUGE trash problem. When Maher first began, the surrounding area had trash in the roads, along roadsides, in fields, everywhere (plastics, food waste, human excrement, etc.). This is a breeding ground for diseases not to mention unpleasant. As part of hygiene improvement, Maher began to build toilets and bore wells, including teaching the people how to care for and keep these clean.

Also through Swachata Program Maher leads programs about planting "kitchen gardens," and how to use garbage. Wet garbage can be composted; dry garbage can be burned; other items can be reused. They help start vermiculture pits (compost) for clean safe handling of household food waste to use as free fertilizer for their kitchen gardens, and handling of animal manure to make free fertilizer for the fields. An additional project is turning human waste into biogas. The trash problems are much reduced now in the areas where Maher has projects.

Solar panels as well as solar-powered hot water tanks adorn the roofs of most Maher Homes and have been installed in villages as well to reduce burning of gas and electricity use, supporting the environment.

Educational opportunities for children (various programs)

Several programs were developed to address the education of children and teens, as well as young people who never attended or failed to complete school. These include kindergartens, day care centers and after-school tutoring. These are described briefly here, then many are shown in action in the stories of work in a slum and the beggars' colony in the next chapter.

Kindergartens (Ushalaya Program) are the foundations of learning. Maher has established kindergartens in remote and distant places which lack facilities for children to access primary education. These schools teach hygiene, often offer at least one warm meal with milk, and begin to teach the basics of numbers and letters. The children learn how to sit in school, be attentive, share, play nicely, and more. Generally, once the schools are up and running, Maher requests that the government take these over and run them so Maher no longer needs to finance these. In the meantime, relationships are built with the families and community linking them to other Maher services.

Daycare centers (Premalaya and Gamat Shala Programs) are established for younger children of working parents. Here the youngest children are taught songs, fed, often clothed, and looked after for the day. Older children (whose parents cannot afford to send them to school) might attend classes structured more like schools so the children pick up the habit of going to school regularly and learn a few things. If they show interest and ability Maher might then sponsor these older children for more formal education.

These schools or daycare centers are brought right into the slums, beggars' colony, or remote areas where the families live. The parents work long hours doing menial, unpredictable labor and could never afford to send their children to any school, let alone feed them sufficiently. Normally the children are left home alone or to wander the streets and fend for themselves while their parents work. At least some of the smaller children later attend Maher kindergartens and some perhaps later, with Maher's assistance, attend public schools.

Maher also offers after-school tutoring in the slums, both to support children to be successful with their schoolwork, but they also receive a light meal and are supervised since the parents would not be home until very late.

Kalasagar - adult education

Most of the adult women who came to Maher with their children never completed school. Several expressed the desire to learn to read, write, and even earn a high school equivalency certificate. These early requests led to the creation of this program.

Kalasagar is an "open school" to earn high school equivalency for those who either never attended school or did not complete school. This allows them to then pursue technical training so they can get better jobs. Often girls in particular are either denied school completely, or only allowed a few years. After that they are kept home to attend to smaller children, attend to flocks in the fields, or be married off while still children themselves. This project is aimed to both raise awareness of the value of education for girls and boys, and to help these adults earn some certification and give them the means for fulfilling their dreams.

Technical and vocational training, plus job placement

There are several programs at Maher aimed at helping residents and villagers gain training for skilled work. One key program is Parishram, which means "hard work". This program began at Maher's original location where the women learned to make crafts. The card-stitching, candle-making etc., was soothing to do for women recovering from trauma and the end products were well-made and salable.

The program is very popular and has been replicated at all Maher centers. The women and teens work hard and create wonders such as different kinds of stitched cloth bags, paper bags, crochet bags, scented candles, hand-stitched cards, photo frames, files, diyas (clay vessels used in Hindu ceremonies), jewelry, masalas (spice and tea mixtures), chocolates and more. Each worker is paid per piece for each item they create. This money is deposited into a bank account for each person so they can build up savings for personal use. The products and items made here are later sent for sale, the proceeds of such sales goes to support Maher's work.[4]

Parishram has expanded beyond simply a production unit into a training center for many women and girls who come from the local and neighboring villages. They receive training in different livelihood courses such as tailoring or beautician and earn a certificate. Afterwards they can start their own small business. There is a huge demand for skills development training as more and more women want to be financially independent or bring an extra income to their families. Maher also sends skilled teachers out to villages and remote areas to teach the classes such as tailoring or beautician or computer skills. According to Maher records, between 1997 and 2020, at least 540 such training programs were held, with nearly 6000 participants.

Faiza's story
This story was shared by Maher staff.

Faiza was an orphan. Both her parents passed away when she was a child. She was raised at an NGO in Pune. She was later sent for nursing classes but she did not complete the course as she was not interested. Then this NGO sent her to Maher as she had problems adjusting to people and places.

---

[4] Not only are these products popular in India, but they are very popular with visitors to Maher. Many of us bring home a suitcase full to give as gifts or sell to benefit Maher. They are always on offer when Sister Lucy is a guest speaker in U.S. and Europe.

Once at Maher she enrolled in BCom (Business Communication, a four-year degree).

While doing BCom she also completed Maher's Greeting Cards training course and Paper Bag training course. She was very good at painting and she beautifully painted the paper gift bags with Warli[5] art or scenery. She completed her four-year degree.

Faiza wrote: "I was confused what education and career I should pursue but with the expert career guidance I received at Maher, today I am able to pursue my dreams. I passed first year exams [in BCom] with very good percentage. I am very glad for the opportunity given to me by Maher to "earn while I learn." I receive a stipend of Rs.1000-1500 per month from making greeting cards, paper bags, and painting in my free time, which I use for my personal expenses and traveling [to classes]. I enjoy what I do and I am very happy here. I am ever grateful to Maher who has made this possible for me."

Swavalamban: Self-help groups

Hira came to Maher about a year after it began. She had a master's in social work (MSW) and had studied self-help groups. She was keen to add this to Maher's programs and Sister Lucy agreed.

Swavalamban means "self-reliance". The project consists of generating and sustaining self-help groups (SHGs) in the villages near all Maher centers. Self-help groups serve multiple purposes simultaneously. Ultimately, they are a

---

[5] Warli designs are a stylized form of tribal painting common in Maharashtra.

means to raising wealth for the women and improving the lives and security of all their families, but through the process the women become more confident, skilled, and even influential in the direction of village development. (And later there have been a few SHGs for teens and men too.)

The aim of self-help groups is to promote financial growth in villages through education, community investment, and loan programs. Maher staff recognized that village women often do not have sufficient resources to meet the needs of their families. It is common for poor rural people to be charged high interest loans from money lenders, resulting in debt that is difficult to repay. Banks will not even consider small loans to poor people. Self-help groups encourage financial independence through education, savings, member loans, and affordable loan repayment. Additionally, Maher has found that family problems, including domestic violence, decrease as the women become income generators which raises up the whole family.

Self-help groups are often introduced after developing relationships from a series of awareness meetings. Sister Lucy, social workers (and sometimes housemothers) do the outreach and start-up which includes explaining the purpose, rules, and structure of a self-help group. They also provide on-going support for these groups. Eventually these groups can take on broader purposes than just promoting financial growth.

First the self-help groups create a space where a group of women living in the same village sit together and collectively discover solutions to their problems and provide support to each other in their time of need. Each month every woman puts in literally pennies at first, collecting these into a small pool. They decide together how to spend this money for the needs of members of the group in the form of small loans. They might choose to loan to one woman to purchase medicine, another to buy a couple of chickens, another to purchase cloth for stitching. These women pay back the loan with a little bit of interest, and so the pot of money grows.

Maher social workers work very closely with each group, teaching them record keeping, collective decision making, conflict resolution skills, as well as leadership and organizational skills. These groups help the women dream of, and create, better lives for the whole village. They learn to design programs and plans for the development of the village, build a shared well, or even a school. Being a part of the group also gives the members a sense of responsibility and builds their confidence. Leaders are identified among the group. SHGs have helped many to start income generation activities such as goat farming, buying cattle, provision shops, cloth shops, papad making (a bread type), paper plate making, etc. Together these women learn to stand up for themselves and their children and the men respect them more as the women become significant contributors to family well-being. Abuse becomes rare.

Self-help groups are one of the most significant tools Maher has brought to village development. These began as micro-finance groups, but also came to serve as support groups for the women. helping one another during crisis. SHGs often take over organizing awareness programs on health, education, superstitions, equality, domestic violence, alcoholism, female feticide, caring for the environment, and more, per the needs of their village.

Now women come to Maher asking for help in establishing local self-help groups. As the earlier groups become firmly established and need less guidance from Maher, the social workers are able to expand the self-help groups further into the interiors of India to new villages where there is great need.

Before Maher however there were no such groups in this region of India so the people had no idea what they were. The story of starting the very first one is fascinating, and they took off from there. (Maher supports over 800 self-helps groups as of 2023.)

Sister Lucy top center, leading a meeting of a village SHG, surrounded by three male social workers. Hira is here also, seen from the back on far-right side. (author's photo)

Story of the first self-help group as told by Hira, with further examples from other self-help groups.

The story of starting the very first SHG is fascinating. This story was told by Hira, one of Maher's first social workers, now Maher's Executive Director.

"When I came to Maher, I knew I wanted to begin to develop self-help groups (SHGs) in the villages. To start, I chose Sangamvasti a small vasti near Vadhu.[6] This vasti was very poor, barely surviving. All were illiterate. They did not even know how to count money. When they went to the shops in the nearby village, the shopkeepers would cheat them because they did not know the difference between ten rupees and twelve rupees. If a person had medical bills or other larger expenses, they had to go to a money lender who charged ten percent or more interest. If they could not pay it back, they could lose their home, their land, everything. Therefore, the people were getting poorer even though they worked very hard. Some even committed suicide when they could not pay the money lender, leaving the entire family destitute.

"A SHG was a totally new idea for the villagers: no one had any idea of how these groups would benefit them. I had to slowly, slowly, gain their trust, explain the SHG, its benefits and how they worked. I began going several times a week,

---

[6] A "vasti" is a collection of about 30-35 families, several vasti together make up a village. This particular one is about 30 minutes by car today.

week after week, to meet the people and slowly gain their trust. It took six months like this to even establish that first SHG!

"Another challenge was that the women worked in the fields all day. I could not meet with them until they were home from the fields and the wives had cooked the food and fed the men. So, sometimes with Sister Lucy or Anand and sometimes alone, I would leave Maher about six in the evening to walk to Sangamvasti, well over an hour's walk. Then I could start to meet with people about nine o'clock at night – according to the local schedule. I went house to house, family to family until sometimes eleven or twelve at night! Then I had to either sleep over or make my way home on foot late at night. In those days, Maher had no car or motor scooter and there were no roads into this vasti."

Slowly, slowly – a unique trademark of Maher's work

"In those days no one knew Maher or Sister Lucy or me. The people were highly suspicious. What were we doing here? Men were worried what are we teaching the women? Maybe we would be teaching the women opposite to what the men teach. Therefore, Maher had to develop good relationships with the men also, to build trust with everyone in the village. Slowly. Slowly. I spoke with the husbands and told them about the SHG and how it would help the whole village. Until the men agreed, the women could not meet. I knew the SHG's should be for the women, run by the women, but we had to have the men with us, or the women would not be allowed to come.

35

"When there was enough interest, Sister Lucy and I invited all the people together for the first meeting, men, women, even the children. The meetings would begin after nine in the evening, after dinner, and last sometimes until midnight or one AM. In front of everyone, we explained again what SHG's were, how they worked, how these would benefit the village."

Story-telling simplifies concepts and builds trust

"To help them understand more about the usefulness of the SHG's, we told stories. Like one family needed to marry their daughter but were poor so they took a loan, could not pay it back, and they lost everything and were even poorer. We told how the SHG was a solution to this problem. We talked to them about families who were saving their money, able to have a small marriage, and so they did not need to go to a money lender. So now this family's future is bright. We used role plays to help them understand. Through the stories and role plays they discovered answers to their own problems. This was far better than us just telling them what to do.

"There were many meetings about this. Slowly the people began to understand and to trust. Only after all this could we bring the women together to meet. Before we came, the people of this vasti would only come together in rare times, like someone dying, or a marriage. They had no tradition of helping each other. The first step was to get the women to sit together for half hour, an hour. Six months from my first visit, after months of slowly building trust and understanding, the first SHG started here with eleven women. By the end of the first year there were twenty women."

Slowly, slowly for the first two years

"We began teaching them decision making, the SHG rules, and to explain again how things work. The women had to agree to come together for one hour at least once a month. The first contributions were just five rupees per woman per month. The people are very poor, so we had to start small. Over time, the group members could agree to slowly raise the monthly contributions.

"Ultimately the SHG's make their own rules. Maher helps them with values in general, and suggests rules that have worked, but each SHG decides for themselves. We are there ultimately to guide them so they can be independent of Maher.

"These groups need written records, yet no one could read, write or do numbers, nor do simple addition and subtraction. I started a simple literacy class for this group. I taught them how to count money, make change, how to read and write a little bit. Even with this, they were not so easily cheated by the shop keepers!

"The next step for the SHG was to open a bank account for the group's money. These people knew nothing about banks. I taught why a bank account is useful, how to open an account, how to put in and take out money, how to keep the records, etc. The group elected president, treasurer and secretary, and we started training these people in the banking.

"All of this took a long time. After two years they could do a little bit of reading, writing, and counting. They learned to write minutes of each meeting – what happened first, second, etc. They learned to track and report on who has paid in money, who has borrowed, and how it was being repaid. We designed a simple process for this.""

Hira spoke more about how the SHG's in general affect the women members and life in their villages.

Before, the banks and money lenders had so many papers and formalities that the people could never understand exactly what was going on. With the SHG these women were in charge together. The women learned to sit, discuss needs and then decide together who should get a loan for what. For example: one woman's daughter was sick, another woman needed money for school fees, another for the farm; different needs, different amounts. As a group they had to assess which needs were most immediate. Together they decided. And the interest on these small loans from the group is much lower: only one to two percent, paid back into the SHG. This way all their money stayed in the vasti.

Maher also spoke with the banks and the government, telling them about the SHG's. We invited the bank people to come to some of the SHG meetings, to explain how the banks could work with them. For example, if a SHG raised 6000 rupees for a project and if it was well-planned, then the bank would provide a matching bank loan. The bank would still charge interest, but at a much better rate than the money lenders. Once SHG's were established and working well, the banks helped with these bigger loans.

Village growth plus more independence and respect for the women

Previously the women had no access at all to money; they had to ask the men even for money to buy milk. Through the SHG the women in the village started and ran small businesses. When a woman started earning, then the family respected her more, and treated her better. The women started small. They bought chickens or a goat, or a water buffalo, for example. This way they raised food plus had some left to sell. They saved what they earned, got another goat (for example), and slowly their businesses grew. Another lady started a small shop, selling grains, candy, a little bit of everything so village people did not have to travel so far for basic things. Later she used a loan from the SHG to expand her business. Another lady started a bangle shop; every woman needs bangles![7]

Before the SHG, no one had money to send their children to school. The children were either left alone during the day or worked in the fields with their parents. Maher also offered awareness raising programs here, where we explained the value of education for girls and boys. After the SHG, the families were not so poor. They saw the value of education and began sending their children to school. With Maher's help, some even went to school outside the local village to study beyond tenth standard. Many of these people had never left the village area all their lives. Today some of these very children have even studied abroad!

---

[7] Bangles are the 'stacks' of narrow bracelets many Indian women wear.

The SHG taught the value of working together to resolve shared problems

SHGs became central to the development of the whole village. In addition to the business of the SHG, the women discussed life in the village and what might make things better for their families. They learned it was very helpful to share a problem, hear others' ideas, and ultimately make a better decision. This was entirely new to the village. Before this everyone made decisions on their own. After, through the SHGs they discussed what was best, for themselves, and also for the village if others were affected. The SHGs taught the power of collective decision-making and gave them practice how to do this. As the women gained independence, skills, and confidence, they began to collectively solve problems; they started planning changes and improvements for their village.

Before and after examples from this first vasti

Before the SHG, there was no water: the well was broken and filled with garbage. After the SHG the village worked very hard together to clean out the well. They raised the money themselves and had the bore well fixed. Now they have water.

Before the SHG, if a woman had trouble at home, she would suffer in silence. After the SHG, the women supported each other. For example, if a woman's husband was giving her trouble she came to the group and spoke up. The whole group then went to the man to try to reason with him. The whole village came to know if there was a problem and this shamed the man. Everyone knew that if he did not shape up, she could go to Maher. The SHG together took the first step of trying to improve things so the family could be safe and stay together. Also, the men began to see the women differently, they saw how life was improved by the work of the women.

Before the SHG, villagers had to spend their hard-earned money outside the village for food, for grinding their grains, etc. Maher explained that money coming into the village should not go out of the village or else the village would not thrive. After the SHG the women started more small businesses in their own village: shops, a local grinding mill, etc. More of their hard-earned money stayed local.

Before the SHG there was no road into the vasti. After, working together, they petitioned the government for a road to the village and later for drainage along the road to avoid the annual flooding of the road. Another village even got a nice new school built by the government. Small things, step by step to make life better. These were possible because the people came together.

Gradually the SHGs began to ask Maher for more awareness raising meetings on issues of special interest for them such as health, legal aid, education, and many more subjects. They began to help Maher plan these. Over time they also brought larger programs to the villages, such as Maher-led International Women's Day celebrations where there were multiple programs and many more exposure groups. They could also request a library, or occupational training, such as tailoring, or beautician, or help creating compost and biogas projects, and more.

The SHG women learned they could act on an even bigger scale

In one area, the women of several SHG's from nearby villages came together. They wanted to stop all the drinking and liquor. They knew that when one person in the family drank this affected the whole family. The men spent all their money on liquor instead of bringing home money for food. The men did not want to pay for the children's education; they wanted only liquor. In that way the whole family suffered. These SHG women banded together. They gave letters to police stations and local government. They explained they were holding a big rally to stop the liquor and drinking. Because of the rally all the liquor shops were closed. They convinced the government to stop liquor licenses at least for a while. The store owners got very angry. The politicians got angry at the SHG's and at Maher. (Maher by no means instigated this, we had only responded to questions from the women). One village leader tried to threaten the SHG and the women beat him up! The liquor stores serving this cluster of villages moved out to the far edges of town. Life in the villages became very nice. The police stood up for the women and protected them from violence. For one or two years most of the drinking stopped. Now the government is again giving licenses to liquor stores but requiring that the liquor shops must not be on the main roads; they must be at least 500 meters back.

Vehicles for social change

Another powerful effect of the SHG's has been to soften the rigidity of the caste system. Villages have different castes and often different religions too. For example: a low caste person makes shoes, a higher caste person might own a shop. But they are all in the SHGs together, across castes and religions, so they get used to working together. In Apti village, for example, Hindus are of the higher castes, and Muslims the lower castes. After many years of SHG's and working with Maher, the mindsets are changing. Recently the village elected a Muslim woman as their new 'Mayor'! She is respected even though she is in the minority religion and lower caste. This author finds this is even more amazing given the current context of greatly heightened religious (Hindu-Muslim) violence being spread across India!

The SHGs spread

As the women talked to other women, for example at a central grinding mill, or in the fields, then women from other vastis and villages began to learn about the SHGs. They then asked for Maher to help them start a SHG. And so the SHGs spread.

From this first SHG, they expanded to every area village, often more than one group per village if it was a larger village. From only myself, after 20 years, there were forty-two social workers and para-social workers supporting over 610 SHGs. Now there are close to 900 SHGs! The SHGs also expanded to everywhere Maher has centers. Every single one became a source of women's empowerment. As Maher expands into new states (three new states in just 2022) the SHGs will spread as well.

At first Maher's social workers supported all of the SHGs. As the sense of empowerment grew, and as education and literacy grew, some of the villagers took Maher's one-year para-social worker training. After completion they were hired to support a cluster of twenty to thirty SHGs in that area. This way Maher staff travelled less, saved money, and at the same time the village became even more self-sufficient. Additionally, when the para-social worker was from the local area, and made suggestions, the people were more likely to listen and respect "one of theirs" even if they were from the next village over. Maher social workers continued to check up on the SHGs regularly, just to be sure everything was going well. Staff responded to requests and questions and supported the para-social workers as they got started.

One final note about results in Vadhu Budruk village

When Lucy opened Maher's first Home here domestic violence was common, as in most of India, and considered the private business of the husband. While technically illegal, no one, including police, responded to women's cries, let alone tried to save her from death.[8] Now, 25 years later, domestic violence in Vadhu and surrounds is exceedingly rare, if it ever happens. There are social and legal repercussions. Family and neighbors look down on the man

---

[8] You may recall the grisly event that led Sister Lucy to start Maher when a woman denied shelter at a convent was burned to death by her husband, along with their unborn baby, Sister Lucy tried but was unable to save her.

who hits his wife. Police and neighbors will intervene. Women understand their rights, and the village respects these rights. Any woman can come anytime to Maher with her children. If a woman goes to Maher, everyone knows why and the husband is shamed. Slowly the culture of violence and a highly patriarchal society has changed; relationships are safer and more respectful; children are safer, happier and even all the girls attend school. Additionally, the economic well-being of all has improved. This area has also managed not to fall prey to the inter-religious hatemongering so prevalent in much of India these days; Hindus, Muslims, Christians live and work together peacefully. In many ways Maher has created oases of mostly peaceful living in a country currently awash in violence. And because Maher is there to stay, as opposed to "helicoptering in" these changes have the best chance of lasting over time. A whole generation has grown up with new values and new opportunities. These results are due to the wholistic approach of Maher and this Patchwork Quilt of programs.

SUMMARY

The above Patchwork Quilt of programs represent tools which are all ways Maher reaches out beyond its gates. Maher is able to do this due to a pool of highly dedicated social workers (MSWs), para-social workers, supervisors and more. It takes special MSW's and professionals who see the ideals and potential of Maher and are willing to forgo the larger city salaries and "live" their work. These professionals must embrace all Maher's values, eat food and live in proximity with people of all castes (including untouchables) and all religions. Additionally, a number of women rescued from the streets have accepted Maher's offer of education and achieved certification as teachers and para-social workers to help take Maher's vision and values out into the villages and slums. Maher's staff, both men and women, is extraordinary. Now some of the children of Maher have grown up, attended University and are back at Maher as staff, even a board member. Many other "alumni" of Maher regularly "tithe" back to Maher whatever they can afford.

Because of this patchwork of programs, the numbers of residents at Maher, which is typically reported to donors, has grossly understated the broad impact of Maher from every site. For example, in the case where two generations of a family are given food and medical care, while one child was brought to Maher to live and go to school, only the one child would be counted in Maher Shelter Home statistics. Or Rachel's family's case where food provisions helped a family of five remain in their home, none of these would have counted in Maher's typically reported numbers. This volume tells the broader story.

In the next chapter you will read about a few specific examples of populations in need, and how Maher applied all these tools to meet the needs in the villages and vastis where the people live.

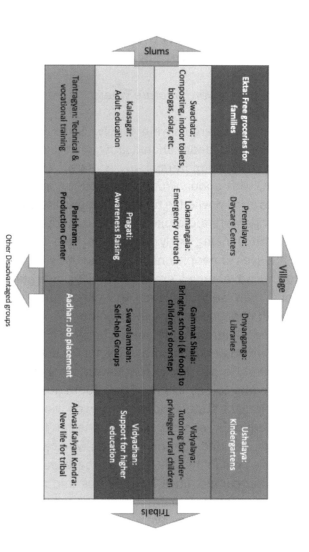

Slums

Ekta: Free groceries for families

Swachata: Composting, indoor toilets, biogas, solar, etc.

Kalasagar: Adult education

Tantragyan: Technical & vocational training

Premalaya: Daycare Centers

Lokamangala: Emergency outreach

Pragati: Awareness Raising

Parishram: Production Center

Village

Dnyanganga: Libraries

Gammat Shala: Bringing school (& food) to children's doorstep

Swavalamban: Self-help Groups

Aadhar: Job placement

Ushalaya: Kindergartens

Vidyalaya: Tutoring for under-privileged rural children

Vidyadhan: Support for higher education

Adivasi Kalyan Kendra: New life for tribal

Other Disadvantaged groups

Tribals

2: VILLAGE DEVELOPMENT:
Bringing Education and Opportunities to Villages, Slums and Disadvantaged Areas.

We walk together toward a future where there is no longer a need for Maher.

Coming from a large loving family, Sister Lucy always believed every child ideally should grow up at home with both parents, even grandparents, in a safe, clean, loving environment, with enough food and clothing, go to school, and get skills and knowledge for a meaningful life. Maher was for when things were too broken for this to happen.

She began thinking early on how to help stabilize and improve the lives of people and families in the villages, slums and other disadvantaged areas. If families are stable and prosperous, can send children to school, and can deal together with challenges, etc., then women would not need or wish to flee, children would not be begging on the streets, and no one would need to come to Maher for shelter.

While poverty is certainly a root cause of much suffering, Sister Lucy came to see illiteracy as a root cause of a lot of poverty, prejudice, superstitions, and even violence in the home. Consequently, she developed a passion for educating children. This included not only the ones who came to live at Maher, but also out in the villages, the tribal areas, the slums, migrant worker camps, brick layer camps and more. As you read in the prior chapter, Maher developed a host of projects aimed toward educating every child they could. These included pre-schools and kindergartens, both for young children and special programs for older children who had never attended school to help prepare them, and also summer vacation programs, tutoring, adult literacy, and more.

Sister Lucy trained some of the women (and a couple of Sisters who later joined her) to help in the care of the children and other women residents. Then she was able to hire Hira and Anand, the first two social workers. This freed up time for Sister Lucy and staff to continue to build from the "patchwork quilt" of services and deepen the relationships in nearby villages. Also, when a wife fled to Maher with her children seeking safety, if the woman sought reconciliation, Maher went into her village to work with the families involved. Often issues involved dowries, caste, poverty, superstitions, as well as abuse. During this process of reconciliation, Maher worked respectfully with the family, but also often with neighbors, village leaders, or police. Maher's reputation grew and more trust was built.

As these relationships developed, Maher was able to take a more "whole village" approach. As Maher is engaging with villagers and families through reconciliations or the "patchwork quilt" of services, they develop relationships, noticing other needs in the village to improve life for other women and children, and for the village as a whole. For example, if the women must go a long way for water, then they might offer to build a well. Or if there are very few jobs or access to work, Maher might begin a self-help group (SHG) for the women to pool resources and help each other solve problems. Even now with all their experience, Maher staff never go to a village and start offering solutions; they listen, they observe, they "see how it is." What do the villagers think they need most? What do they think their challenges are?

With what do they need help? What solutions have they tried and what happened? What other solutions or actions are they thinking about? No assistance is offered by Maher in a "one size fits all" formula; aid is always based on this listening and learning.

ONE RELATIONSHIP, ONE VILLAGE AT A TIME

Below are some examples of these efforts, applied together, to bring education, opportunities and a better life to a community. Apti represents a typical village, where Maher tried a new experiment in village development. The other three examples below are especially disadvantaged groups: Perne Phata Slum, a local beggars' colony, and a nearby tribal community.

Example of Apti

Apti village today is about 15 minutes by scooter from Vadhu Center, Maher's first Center and base. Here Maher tried yet another innovation: embedding the social worker in the village. When interviewing candidates with master's degrees in social work, Maya Shelke (MSW) said she wanted to live in and work with a whole village: a children's home, self-help groups, awareness raising, all the programs the village might need for its development. Sister Lucy agreed. Maher had already begun building relationships here through the patchwork quilt of services and thought this village would be a great place to begin.

Maya began developing her own relationships with the people. With the agreement of the village, Maher built a small residential children's home and Maya moved in. Sister Lucy sent some of the small orphan children (first to fourth standard) and a housemother from Vadhu to live in this new home with Maya. There was a government village school here by now, so the children from Maher attended school with the local children. As Maya listened and learned the people's needs, Maher built toilets for the school. More SHGs were started, with Maya supporting all of them. Eventually in addition to the SHGs for women, they started groups for men and for teenagers, at the people's requests. All the principles of collective decision making, conflict resolution, record keeping, activities, etc. were learned and used in these groups as well. As conflicts arose in the village, Maya helped sort things out. She organized awareness programs and also festivals such as International Women's Day.

As these skill sets rose across the village, domestic violence became nearly non-existent, caste and religious barriers fell. Even with the recent rise in Hindu Nationalism, peace has reigned in Apti. In fact, recently the village elected a Muslim woman as Mayor! (Culturally, Muslims are seen as lower caste in India, and women are rarely elected to positions of power.) It is through the SHGs that the people became used to trusting and working closely with all their neighbors regardless of gender, caste, or religion. Sister Lucy is respected as an elder of the village, though she does not live there.

Maya, as social worker, was also responsible for programs for the sugar cane migrant families when they were there during sugar cane harvest. (Laborers and their families travel farm to farm harvesting this major Indian crop.) These workers lived in temporary "tents" and their children either remained in the tents or came to the fields. Maya and Maher established a day care for these children. They were fed, enjoyed organized activities, and gained a bit of education. Maya also organized basic awareness programs like hygiene and the value of literacy. Families were assisted with food, clothing and blankets as needed.

Apti is now a thriving village. With over 20 years at Maher, Maya has become a senior social worker. Later her husband Adul left his business job, completed social work training, and joined Maher staff as a social worker.

The principles of village development apply to other groups, though the following three groups have unique features and needs requiring unique adaptations and approaches. The more disadvantaged and remote, the less trust in outsiders.

Perne Phata Slum

The Perne Phata slum area is in Wagholi, just outside of Pune. Maher staff and guests pass the entrance to this slum every day traveling from Vadhu (original and main Maher site) on the way to Maher's Pune office. This slum therefore seemed a natural place to extend Maher's offerings. Here too parents are gone long days (even nights) working or begging. If they do work, it is often as day laborers: the men and women looking for day work amass at a given road intersection and wait, hoping to be picked for the day. If they are not picked (and many are not) then they have no work and no way to feed their families. It is very irregular work. Or they might pick through roadside trash for bits of salvageable items, such as cloth for rags (hence the name "ragpickers"). Alcoholism, drug abuse, and domestic violence are common in these communities, as is despair. Most of the adults are illiterate. The children are left alone for long periods, or perhaps a granny might live with them. Education is a distant dream.

Maher started with the children. Sister Lucy or staff came in the mornings after the parents had left and brought a warm breakfast and milk to pass out. Often this was the only food these children ate all day. Slowly Maher became known and trusted.

Soon, a bit of space inside the slum was given to Maher to erect a three-sided tin shed to start a kindergarten and day care. They focused on children one to eight years old. They began with food, hygiene, and fun-based learning, including numbers and the alphabet. This helped the children prepare for school in the future: children unused to any structure in their days have a difficult time sitting still for a period of time – a necessary skill to attend a real school in the future.

It did not take very long before the whole slum came to know Maher and Sister Lucy. As the kindergarten program grew and more children attended, it became clear they were ready for more. With parental approval, groups of children were invited to Maher for a month over the school holiday season. (Maher rotated different communities of children through each vacation season.) In this way, at least some of the children were readied for more formal schooling. Some even came to live at Maher for the school year, visiting their parents for holidays and breaks. The parents were invited to visit on Sundays (school in India runs Monday through Saturday) and for big programs. In this way, slum children began getting educations, then jobs, and new dreams.

Maher is well-known and respected, and Sister Lucy is loved and welcomed in the slum. As this author toured the slum with Sister Lucy, I saw how the women there tried so very hard to keep their homes neat and clean. These homes were often rags draped over sticks with a dirt "floor." The lucky ones had a bit of tin for a roof to keep out the rain in the rainy season. A fortunate family might have a goat for milk who shares this hut with the family. The animal droppings were mostly picked up and even the dirt floors had clearly been swept. People had pride in the little they had – and they always offered to share a bit of something, even to people like me! There is a deep sense of hospitality and generosity in the Indian people. Sister Lucy explained that Maher taught about hygiene and the people have mostly embraced it.

It used to be that children born in the slums lived their whole life there. Now, thanks to Maher, they have a road out into better lives.

Beggars' Colony

The Pardhivasti community in Shirur District (about an hour by jeep from Vadhu) had no water, no electricity; the homes were crude and crumbling. There was little if any awareness of personal hygiene practices, healthcare or nutrition. The adults and children were all illiterate. The parents went out daily and were gone long hours into the night, wherever they could find work or begging. Their children were left alone, uncared for, and ran wild. Often each household had seven to twelve children. Maher first tried to repair some of the houses, but they were quickly ruined again. The people were not ready for this.

Maher wanted to help the children, so as in the slum, they began bringing food and treats for the children, met some of the parents, and began to build trust. Here too the next step was to build a simple three-sided shed, offering warm food, milk, and some fun-based learning activities. Gradually as Maher built trust, they added hygiene, clean clothing, and other essential life skills. They began to teach letters and numbers too.

One of the early challenges was that the two teachers would get nauseated because the children smelled so bad. Maher installed a bore well with a hand pump next to the shed-school and hired two more people to help. These two went early, collected all the children, gave them each a "bath" at the new hand pump, and dressed them in clean clothes the staff brought. Then the children went to Maher's school for breakfast and the school day. At the end of the day, the children returned the clothes to the two Maher helpers who took the clothing home and washed them for the next day.

This went on for a few years and slowly Maher gained the trust of the adults too. They too began to practice better hygiene. At about this time, this author visited this village. I motioned to ask if I could take a photo of some of the people. One woman waved at me to wait. Then she hurried to the well with her little boy and washed his face, hands, and combed his hair! Now she was ready! Sister Lucy smiled broadly at this, telling me this was a sure sign of progress – pride in cleanliness!

This same visit Sister Lucy started asking the parents if any would let their children come to Maher for a month in the school vacation season for learning, sports, etc. The time for this was still a few months away. Staff and the teachers continued to talk about it with both the adults and the children. Finally, a group of children and their parents agreed. Maher had space and time for this because so many of Maher's resident children go home to their parents or other relatives for school vacation.

When the children of Pardhivasti arrived at Maher's Vadhu center it was a big culture shock to them. One example was using an inside toilet; they were used to squatting on the ground wherever they felt like it. At Maher they were expected to go into a small room, close the door and squat over a porcelain Indian toilet. Then they were supposed to use the water spigot inside to wash themselves with water and to use the bucket provided to wash down their wastes. They had never seen such a thing. The children were frightened, so they would squeeze in, four or five at a time, and take turns once inside!

Staff allowed this to happen and let the children adjust over time. Maher was wise to bring these children in when most of the Maher children were away. Otherwise, Sister Lucy explained, they would have been laughed at and ridiculed by children who were used to toilets. Children are children!

These children had also never lived according to any schedule, except the hours in Maher's "school." They slept when they were tired, woke when they felt like it, ate when they were hungry and could find something, and ran around when and where they liked. In contrast, daily life at Maher is fully structured. The children wake up at five-thirty AM, have a bath (often at an outdoor water spigot), brush their teeth, put on clean clothing, have breakfast, etc. The time is organized all day: sports, classes, meditation, playtime, meals, cleaning clothes, etc. until bedtime at nine or ten PM depending on their age. Maher has learned that especially street and slum children need lots of activities to fill their time or they will get into way too much mischief.

Slowly these children adapted, relaxed and had fun. They were eager to return the next year. After two years a tremendous change has been noticed. The children now are confident and eager to attend regular schools and there is also a change in the outlook of the whole Pardhivasti community towards education and better living conditions.

Working Within the Tribal Areas

Maher has worked with tribal peoples in both Maharashtra and Jharkhand. The tribal peoples are at the very most bottom rung of Indian social structure, even below the "Untouchables." They live in remote areas usually completely without government services or even roads. Often there is no legal recognition that they even exist. There have been some government laws giving tribals certain rights, but generally none of them know about these laws in order to claim their rights. They are illiterate, desperately poor, and even their spoken language is often unique to their tribe, further isolating them.

Sister Lucy came to hear of one such vasti nearby and determined to meet them and learn how Maher could help.

Both Sister Lucy and Hira told parts of this story of working with the first tribal group, including some of the individual stories of people from this vasti. Some of the older current residents contributed comments about what it was like before Maher and how it is now.

Displaced from their ancestral land

Thakars are tribal people. They were forced from their ancestral lands when a big company built a dam. They lost their land, homes, everything. They migrated looking for work. A big landowner here offered jobs to work in the fields and allowed the Thakars to stay and build huts on a part of his land. The Thakars therefore do not own their land. But now they have been staying here for many years (forty years or so Maher estimated) so no one can send them away. "Their legal address shows here." Sister Lucy explained. The people did not know this; this is one of their rights which Maher taught them.

"We see how it is"

As with any new relationship, Maher began by "seeing how it is." Maher never comes in telling people what to do or how to live. When Maher first went to Thakarvasti in about 2000, they were meeting mostly the second generation (i.e.: not the ones who migrated). Only perhaps one or two of the original people were still left. They are the ones who told Maher the story of the dam and being forced from their land. When Maher first met them, the Thakar life span was fairly short since they worked hard, had barely enough food to survive, no medical care (let alone access to education) and alcoholism was high. At this time, there were about 40 to 50 families and 200 people in Thakarvasti.

Sister Lucy explained: "These people spoke their own language, so we did not understand each other easily. It was a challenge to make ourselves understood especially to understand our intentions. People from nearby villages warned them not to trust us, telling them I am a Christian and that I would try to convert them."

Sister Lucy knew that these people were being cheated by the people who hired them. These tribal people were illiterate. They did not know how to count hours, money, anything. The hirers were taking advantage of them. Other people who knew how to count hours and money were getting paid more than these people. Therefore these tribal people were getting poorer and poorer.

This village was a distance away from Maher and the road only went part way. In those days Maher had no jeep. Sister Lucy and Hira had to hike into the vasti in the dark, in danger from snakes, jackals, etc., as well as from rocks thrown by suspicious nearby villagers. Maher could not risk sending one woman alone, so both Sister Lucy and Hira went together, or sometimes Anand (male social worker) and Hira went.

In the words of the people

Some of the older Thakarvasti residents recently reminisced about what life was like before Maher came and what they thought when Maher first showed up. Below are some excerpts from these recollections:

"Our houses were built with branches and mud. We had no water, no electricity and no proper roads. The women had to go a long way daily to fill our water containers, carry it on their heads and bring it home."

This author crawled into one of these "houses" – more like a low dirt cave! Short as I am, I could barely even sit up in the center highest area without hitting my head on the dirt "roof."

"We had no livestock because, even if we could buy one, the water was too far away. Grinding mills, shops were all far away and there was no road to travel easily to another village on foot."

"None of our children went to school and nearly none of the adults were educated either. Often the girls were married by age thirteen; our life-expectancy was not very long."

"We worked in the fields but we were not paid any wages. We lived on boiled onions and potatoes [left over in the fields] because we had no money to buy food grains. Life at that time was really very difficult and uncertain. Even as a granny, I would go to work in the fields daily."

"No one would ever visit our village, so initially we were very scared [when Maher came]. On seeing them we would get frightened and close our doors or hide ourselves behind the trees. Later we gained some confidence and spoke with the Maher people. They truly wanted to know how we lived and what would most help us. They asked about basic facilities and necessities like the children's schooling, proper homes to live, food, electricity and water."

A first step: literacy and basic awareness

Maher decided to first offer an adult literacy class. The Thakar language was only spoken, not written. Hira taught the literacy part while Sister Lucy talked about topics to raise awareness: what happens to you if you are not literate, tribal legal rights from the government, how to fight for your rights, etc.

Hira remembers: "We started gathering the women, but as in other villages we could only talk to them at night. These women too worked all day in the fields. Then they came home and prepared food for their children and husbands. They could only meet after about nine PM. We started with how to count money. We showed them what is one rupee, two rupees, five rupees, ten rupees, and so on. We had the villagers hold the money, count the money – things like that. Then we started showing them the alphabet and numbers, how to write and recognize these. We showed them both in Marathi and Hindi as these languages are very similar, with the same alphabet. Then the men started showing interest and soon they joined the classes."

"In those days," Sister Lucy said, "there were not so many children living at Maher as now. Plus a few of the women were able to help, so we fed and took care of our children and then traveled to this vasti in the evening. We would be there until one AM then have to travel home. This was really taking a toll on our health as we were up early again with our children and working all day."

Through the literacy class Sister Lucy met a man (Sachan) who was originally from this vasti, but now lived in a nearby village. He had a bit of education already (to the seventh standard) but was coming to the literacy class to learn more. Sister Lucy helped him earn his tenth standard (high school equivalency) and then hired him to take over teaching the literacy class.

Later Maher noticed a declining interest in the literacy class. They started experimenting with ways to keep the attendance up in classes. For example, if people came regularly for one month to class, then Maher would give them a steel vessel as a gift (such as a cup or a plate) or maybe a sari, a blanket, or a man's clothing suit.

Further improvements

Next Maher installed a bore well with a hand pump in the vasti so the people had access to water. After the adults were somewhat literate, then Maher began a self-help group. This too helped improve the lives of all the people.

Maher wanted to start a kindergarten for the children but who would teach there? They wanted someone who understood the people. Sister Lucy immediately thought of Sachan. She sponsored him to take the training to get his Kindergarten Teacher Certificate. Then he was hired by Maher as the first teacher at the new kindergarten. Still later Maher gave him the training for para-social worker after which he could lead the area SHG's.

A wedding and a tragedy: Ragini and Sachan's story

Sister Lucy told this story; it still haunts her today.

"We had just started the work in Thakarvasti. I got to know Sachan first through the literacy classes in Kendur (nearby) and then later as he attended in Thakarvasti. He helped the people of Thakarvasti accept us based on his experience of Maher's work in Kendur.

"He was getting married and he invited me to the wedding. I had no idea how a tribal marriage takes place. When I got there I could see that the 'tent' for the marriage was made of leaves. The food was steamed rice with salt and chili powder sprinkled on it. That was the fancy marriage dinner. I was shocked. In Kerala, where I grew up, we would have meat, fish, and so many different dishes. And it was just this steamed rice here! Rice was a rare special food for them, as was any grain. The whole village was invited plus extended family who lived in nearby Kendur.

"There was a ritual where they gave a special bath to the bride-to-be and that's when I first met Ragini. She was so young – not even developed! I had no clue what her age was. I was utterly shocked. I was so sad. I asked her age. They did not even really understand 'age' yet, they were that illiterate. (I later learned she was thirteen.) I learned that in the tribal caste people marry young.

"When I got home, I was so disturbed by the young age of the bride and the extent of the poverty. All were dressed so shabbily; the women wore torn saris (their best). I looked so out of place even in my sari which was not nice enough to have worn to a wedding in Kerala. I was still quite new to Thakarvasti so I hadn't yet realized how extreme their poverty was. Only rice, not even a vegetable. It was a big shock for me.

"I thought about this a lot. What do I do now? This girl was too young to marry! I have to do something!

"I decided the first thing was to teach the people the importance of educating the women. I went again and again to this village. I spent a lot of time with Ragini; she was young and could learn. I taught her the alphabet and sent her to school. Her husband and his parents were willing to allow this: they trusted me. When she was a little educated, I gave her a job where she could run classes for the little children, a day care, in Thakarvasti. We fed these children, too. The people were very happy.

"The couple had two children, a boy and a girl. Then tragedy struck. It turned out that Sachan had taken a big loan – 20,000 rupees – for their marriage. Though he tried for almost five years, he could not pay this back. Because of this he hanged himself. At first, I could not understand why he hanged himself. I had given him small jobs, such as teaching the literacy class and kindergarten teacher. It was enough for their daily expenses. I did not know about the loan. I could have helped him somehow, but he did not tell me. I came to know only after his death.

"When Ragini saw the body hanging like that she got such a shock she lost her hearing. Ragini was so young, even then she was only eighteen, suddenly a widow with two children, and now deaf. I did not know what was going on.

"Once she became deaf, Ragini could no longer teach, so she no longer had a job. Her in-laws threw her and the children out. The Maher social worker told me this. I told them to bring Ragini and her children to Maher. It was a challenge to employ her without hearing. We set her to help in cooking for the children here so she would not feel so discouraged, so she could contribute. She could begin to heal and her children were cared for with us.

"I did not know shock could lead to physical symptoms like this. I took her to the ear doctor. I took her to several doctors. They said all that can be done is to get her a cochlear implant.

This item costs about seven lakhs. [about $1500 USD] I did not know what to do.

"After some time, I told her story to a businessman. He was moved and said he would help. He sent enough money and she got the operation.

"Now Ragini can hear and is teaching kindergarten for Maher in one of the slums. Her children are now teenagers, sixteen and seventeen years old. They are getting well-educated at Maher. Because she is working again and no longer a burden, her own family and her husband's family have accepted her back, so she and the children go there on holidays. She is much happier!"

Village life after Maher: the residents report

The residents previously quoted about life before Maher, also shared some of the changes to their lives through the support of Maher.

"Staff helped us so we could re-build our houses with stones & cement. This happened over time as gradually the situation of each family improved and we were each able to afford to rebuild our houses with proper material."

"The first classes for children were under a tree. Now we have seen our dream of the future realized: all the children are going to a real school and have brighter futures. Those who wish to can even go on to higher education thanks to Maher."

"My daughter was able to complete her Diploma in Education and is now working as a teacher."

"With the help of Maher we started self-help groups, Balwadis (kindergartens) for the little children, study classes for the fourth and fifth standard children and later schooling for the elder children in classes ten through twelve. My brother's daughter became a nurse. Even the elderly learned to sign their names."

"By then, with the help of the Gram Panchayat[9] and the farmers, a proper road was built. This was very useful to us, making it easier to travel and for people to come to us."

"After the village had proper water supply and with the initiative taken by the SHGs, some of the villagers started to keep livestock (goats and chickens). The government also started helping in various ways. A flour mill was started here, so we (and people from other nearby vastis) could grind our wheat and grains. Maher also helped towards start-up of a shop so people could buy their necessities locally. Gradually village life improved. Many of the men were able to buy two-wheelers [bicycles] so they were able to commute and go to the main market to buy vegetables and other items. As more people got two-wheelers and could travel, the shop here has closed."

---

[9] Gram Panchayat is a basic village governing institute in Indian villages. It is a democratic structure at the grass-roots level in India. It acts as a cabinet of the village. They petitioned the government for a road to the village.

"I was only age five when Maher first came, and now, thanks to Maher, and my education, I have become a Upaserpanch of [nearby] Kendur village. In the local government this position is being the second chief person in the village. Because of this I was able to work on behalf of my village."

"Previously people believed in a lot of superstition. If they were sick, they did not go to any hospital. They would go to people who believed in black magic. After a lot of discussions people became more and more aware of situations like child marriage which needed to be stopped immediately and for the children to get a proper education, hygiene etc. Maher taught us how to live a disciplined life."

Further observations from Sister Lucy

"In this way Maher built up a relationship with the people of this vasti and they began to trust us. Then we started to bring some of the children to live at Maher, those who wanted to go for higher schooling. We especially encouraged the girl-children, in order to help with ending the practice of marrying them so young. We would even give some who were clever extra support so they could "jump the class" to catch up with the other girls their age. This is strictly a volunteer basis – the parents and the children must all want to do this. Ragini [from the above story] was one of the first.

When these children returned home on holidays and then after their education, they were so nice, and well set up, and the families were so proud of them. Now we do not have to go ask for them to send the children. For the first fifteen years it was a lot of work and struggle, but now all of the children in this village attend school without us even asking. The parents see the benefits and want this for their children. This is a big change in one generation!"

In about 2004 Maher built a small Home in Thakarvasti where children would come live and attend school, from first standard through eighth standard. After this, these children could go to the Maher Home in Kendur village for eighth through tenth standards. This completed "high school" in India. After this, those who had the ability and desire for more could come to Maher Vadhu and be sponsored for further schooling.

Leela was one of the first girls from Thakarvasti to come to Maher Vadhu after tenth standard. Below is her story.

From bleak poverty to professional nurse to
village leader: Leela's story

Leela wrote up part of her story in English (below) when she was 26 years old. Later Sister Lucy and this author added to it.

"We were very poor and faced extreme poverty. In the year 2005, I came to Maher and lived at the Maher Navjeevan Home in Thakervasti. I was just five years old. I studied there from first through eighth standard. Then I went to Maher's Kendur Home to continue my schooling. I was determined and happy that I was able to complete my tenth standard.

"After I completed my tenth standard, I came to the Aboli Home at Maher Vadhu. I had the opportunity to work in the Production unit and learned to make a lot of products. I was able to adjust to the culture and wanted to study further. I completed my eleventh and twelfth grades and then went to a college in Koregaon. [Larger village near Vadhu.] Later, I did my ANM nursing training at Tarachand Hospital for one and a half years. I was very happy that I was able to complete my course and grateful for the whole-hearted support from Maher."

Sister Lucy inserted that after Leela completed twelfth standard, her parents were pushing to get her married. Lucy convinced them to wait and let Leela get training in a skill for a better job. This way Leela was able to attend nursing training. Then she got a job at the local hospital. After this Sister Lucy told the family that they could arrange a marriage for Leela.

Leela continued: "In 2015 I was pleased to be married to Gaurav. I went to live with him and was a housewife. I was very interested to become a Police Patil, so I completed the application form for the Police Patil exam. I passed the examination and became a Police Patil.[10]

"I received a lot of support from the villagers, did a lot of good work and everyone cooperated with me. I now have two children: a four-and-a-half-year-old son and a one-month-old baby girl. What I am today and all that I could accomplish was

---

[10] Sister Lucy explained this position is a big post. She is a leader in her village, one who looks after the village, a sort of government liaison. If anyone in the village has a problem, they go to her. One example is for help to appeal to the government for aid: Leela needs to write a recommendation letter to the government on their behalf. She organizes many things in her village like that.

only because of the love, encouragement and support I received from Maher."

Sister Lucy summarized: "Leela was the first woman, even the first person, from her village to get this level of education. She was so shy and sweet when I first met her, and each year I would see more confidence and poise in her. Wow!"

This author met Leela in 2010 shortly after Leela came to live in Aboli house. She was very shy. She had only a few words of English and I had only a few in Marathi, but we connected with lots of smiles and hand motions. Leela was always eager to help people. While I was in Pune during the day, she would take my washing off the clothesline and iron it dry for me. (It was the rainy season – nothing really ever dried on the clothesline.) I would find my clothes dry and ironed in my room. She also ironed my sari for me – a most fascinating process to watch. Saris are very long rectangles of cloth 45 inches wide and 15-30 feet long (4.5-9 meters long). There are no ironing boards; she ironed it the traditional Indian way. This is an intricate process of folding, ironing the top bit, refolding and ironing, refolding and ironing, etc. that boggles my mind! How do they know they got it all? But she did! It is extra special to see her now with a husband, a family and taking a leadership role in her village.

SUMMARY OF VILLAGE OUTREACH AND RESULTS

Over the years, Maher has built many "learning centers," such as daycares, preschools and kindergartens, in remote and distant places which lack facilities for children to access primary education. Without this early intervention, these children had little hope of formal schooling. In addition to the communities detailed above, they have served communities of migrant workers, brick kiln workers, and others who camp near the site where they find work.

Whenever possible Maher found teachers who came from the local village where the kindergarten was located, and then trained them at Maher. This helped the parents have confidence and trust in them, so they sent their children and went to work worry-free.

A common element to all of these has been organized activities for the children. In addition to sports and dance, Maher took them on short trips and picnics, even into a city. Such "exposure visits" is another Maher program: the children get exposure to city life which contributes to their self-confidence in the world and brings them joy. Maher also ensured that these children got enrolled in schools. Apart from providing the necessary educational material, Maher also provided snacks and food for the children.

Over time, as parents began to see the benefits of education, some of these children from tribal areas, slums and other especially disadvantages areas were enrolled in local schools. (Maher covered all expenses.) It was important to actively ensure success as these children became the first in their family's history to go to school. Tutors were engaged to provide additional assistance with homework and difficult school subjects such as mathematics and English. Many of these children have now passed tenth, even twelfth, standard and are pursuing further studies. The school dropout rate has also considerably decreased. Parents have begun to take the initiative to send their children to school regularly and on time. Everybody is glad to see the children's progress.

Observations of this author

Sister Lucy's and Maher's relationships with the local villages around Pune have grown from mistrust to respect and partnership. The village leaders, still generally men, have a deep respect for her. They touch her feet when they meet, in India a sign of deep respect toward a teacher. (Though Sister Lucy always playfully asks them not to!) During my most recent trip, the wife of one of the Apti village elders had died. Sister Lucy went to pay her respects, as usual with Hira and a group of foreign guests in tow. We sat with the family in vigil on their front porch and were graciously served chai tea. Several other prominent area men were there as well, all greeting Sister Lucy with respect and deference. (None of these men are Catholic, and most were wearing the traditional white Gandhi suits and hats.)

Another man arrived – the representative from this region in the state government. He too was respectful to Sister Lucy. Hira translated some of the conversation to us. Sister Lucy asked the man from the state government again about aid to Maher for care of all these people. He said essentially that the government does not provide financial assistance to any NGO because the vast majority are corrupt. He says Sister Lucy and Maher are the shining example of what could be and they want to help, but then they would have to give to others who are not good people. Later that evening Sister Lucy told us she knows this; she just brings it up from time to time, because you never know – things change!

I marvel again at Sister Lucy's ability to build relationships. Some of these very men were mistrusting of her and fought the cultural changes she pushed. (For example: re-marriage for widows, educating girl-children, equal rights and justice for women and lower castes.) Life in these villages surrounding Maher's original Vadhu Center is culturally and economically significantly different than before. Even I have witnessed changes in my ten plus years of visits. Maher has led well-attended marches against rape. It is common to see girls riding not only bicycles but also motor bikes now, when neither was allowed even ten years ago. Yet she has done this while building respect and good relations.

3: VALUES-BASED GROWTH AND DEVELOPMENT

VALUES-BASED EARLY OPERATIONS AND THE PATCHWORK QUILT OF SERVICES

Maher's values were not specifically articulated, but simply how Sister Lucy worked. They were inspired by her own deep love and commitment guided by her personal understanding of the example of Jesus's life.[11] Sister Lucy never set these in a list somewhere. Rather, this author, observed these practices when I began following Lucy and learning from her how Maher operated. In 2010 I had been asked to write a handbook enumerating step by step how to create a Maher anywhere in India. This was envisioned as a response to all the people who asked Lucy to build a Maher in their part of India. Lucy wanted to encourage other people to do what she was doing, so she could focus on Maher as it was. *Dignity from Despair* was the result. I listed the values practices that I witnessed over and over. Sister Lucy shared more examples and helped clarify these. They are now included in New Employee Manuals. But to Sister Lucy these are not a page in a book, plaque on a wall, or an afternoon lecture; they are simply her heart in action. She expects all staff to work from these values, regardless in which state of India they are

---

[11] Sister Lucy distinguishes between what her heart tells her Jesus would himself have done, and what the Church hierarchy says one should do.

working. She also guides staff, residents, village self-help group members, to follow these values as they live and deal with each other.

She and staff lead by example. As you read through these values and the examples below, you will also see how they underlie not only the flow of daily life in all Maher homes, but also Maher's Patchwork Quilt of services.

MAHER'S CORE VALUES

These values were, and are, revolutionary in India. Though Lucy is a Catholic nun, all these values are interfaith, which itself is one of the core values. Sister Lucy has spent a great deal of energy over the years to both guide staff and residents in these values, and to spread and nurture them in the surrounding communities. Below each is named, with examples of challenges encountered living and working steadfastly true to these values.

Embracing people of all faiths, regardless of caste, class, or ethnicity

India is a society built on a strict Hindu caste structure, Brahmins at top and Untouchables/Dalits at the bottom. In Hindu-majority areas, further below these are Muslims, orphans and tribals. While on paper the caste system has been abolished at the national level, in practice it is fully active in most of India. There is generally a significant social and economic divide between the upper and lower castes. (Clues to caste are in skin tone and family names. Darker skin tones are generally lower caste.) At Maher, staff hired with professional degrees generally would have been from the higher castes. They would not have had much experience mingling socially with lower castes, let alone living with them and loving and nurturing them. This was too much for some early hires – they refused to even eat off plates that might have been used by an Untouchable, let alone hug them! Sister Lucy learned quickly to describe exactly what was expected of all staff, regardless of degrees, etc.

Maher now has an incredible staff of nearly 200 skilled and dedicated social workers. who are happy to embrace Maher values. However, many found they had to relearn habits and question life-long thought patterns. These amazing people work long hours with less pay than their city counterparts. But they have also reminded this author that they have the joy of seeing children heal and thrive, not just survive. At Maher their work makes a much deeper impact on the people's lives than was possible in previous, more traditional assignments. Maher has learned how to select professional staff who are a good fit for Maher.

Maher has also been able to enroll bright children from lower castes into some of the best English-medium private schools, where normally they would not have been considered, regardless of funding. This is yet another way India's caste system is reinforced and that Maher is working to overcome.

Sister Lucy wants everyone who enters the doors to feel welcome. People entering see the beloved symbol of their own faith on display and feel welcome. All new arrivals are met with an offer of chai tea, food, water, a bath, even before paperwork is completed. "We see how it is; and do the needful." So, at every Maher site, an altar with Maher batik of a flame surrounded by symbols of the 12 most common religions in India is prominent.[12]

Additionally the Chair of the Maher Trust is Muslim and the board is composed of Indian residents of Muslim, Christian and Hindu faiths.

Spiritually-infused interfaith daily life and operations

Sister Lucy is a Catholic nun. The area in which she founded Maher was primarily Hindu and Muslim. Sister Lucy

---

[12] See Appendix 3 for descriptions and meanings of symbols

knew in her heart how her own faith supported her in times of difficulty. How could she expect a woman fleeing for her life to "check her religion at the door" or have to be converted in order to be safe? From the start, she knew Maher had to be interfaith, where all faiths were equally respected and welcomed. Sister Lucy firmly believes there is more than one "right" way to find God. All religions profess love for the Divine. Because Secularism is not a thing in India, being a secular operation was never an option. Every Home has the interfaith altar. There are morning prayers and meditation, meal prayers and more for special occasions. Most are sung, making it easy for the children to learn. All are carefully written to not use any particular name of the Divine, not even "God". There is also time for silent prayer, which each may do according to their own beliefs. Major religious holidays of each of the local religions are actively celebrated, such as Eid, Diwali and Christmas. Everyone, staff and residents, participate. (This expectation also turned away some potential professional staff.) Spiritual principles of each tradition are discussed. Sister Lucy has said that if someone comes to Maher during Christmas, they would think all Maher was Christian; if someone came during Diwali, they would think all Maher was Hindu; and if someone came during Eid, they would think all Maher was Muslim. This has proven both more challenging and yet more rewarding in the context of the current Hindu-majority government and religious unrest.

Another challenge has been keeping to Maher's interfaith commitment when donors want to help but with religious strings attached. For example, a donor was inspired to support Maher's work and offered to send cases of free bibles for the people, along with a cash donation. Sister Lucy could not accept the bibles since that preferenced one religion, so she could not accept the cash that came with them. This donor chose to walk away rather than make the donation without the bibles. Another donor gave a Home, then wanted only one religion there, and even threatened to take back the donated home. Each of these situations had to be carefully handled to maintain Maher's values, treat each donor with respect, and explain Maher's vision. Maher is always prepared to walk away from a gift, even a building, if the donor cannot come to accept Maher ways and core values.

The generation of children who grew up at Maher, while coming from Hindu, Muslim, Buddhist or Catholic families, fully embrace interfaith. Even so, generally they marry within their own faith and caste. Traditionally a bride still goes to live with her husband's family; hence a match in caste and religion gives this living arrangement more chance for success. Still, some of the young people have married each other, for example, a girl from a Hindu family married a boy from a Muslim family. Sister Lucy had many conversations with her family to gain their support so the wedding could take place with both families in attendance.

Unconditional love and respect for all

Sister Lucy exudes unconditional love and everyone who meets her can feel this. This author has witnessed traumatized women, so frightened that they can only whimper, release into Sister Lucy's embrace or finally eat food offered from her hands. Another time a terrified child hid under Sister Lucy's sari when she heard men's voices! She had arrived while Lucy was away and had not yet met her, and still this four-year-old knew she was safe with Sister Lucy.

One way Sister Lucy expresses this love, is that she gives the residents many chances to make mistakes and try again. They make bad choices; Sister Lucy does not judge them. She knows that people who have lived on the streets, or in traumatic homes, have lots of hidden wounds and no real experience with unconditional love. So, like a mother, Sister Lucy helps them learn, lovingly. Almost no one is forced to leave Maher, unless they are a danger to other residents.

New staff need support to live this unconditional love and at the same time to manage the mischief (and worse) street children can get into, or traumatized children having trouble adapting to school, for example. Yes, there are rules and consequences, but Love guides all: love, patience, and multiple chances. India is an authoritarian culture, so this is not how most Indian social workers were trained. Many of these social workers had never experienced unconditional love themselves. Sister Lucy models this to them too, and they also get many chances. Staff and residents both know they can turn to Sister Lucy with their problems or when facing difficult situations. Because Lucy cannot be everywhere at once, she is often on the phone with staff, housemothers, even the women and children, at all hours of the day and sometimes night. When she is in residence in Vadhu, there is often a line outside her bedroom door by six AM!

Another way unconditional respect is embedded at Maher is their insistence to listen first and build relationships before providing help. "We see how it is. Then we do the needful." There is no "one size fits all" for family reunification or village development. Staff will educate and explain to the people what their options are and what outcomes might be expected, but ultimately Maher comes to understand and respect the families' and villagers' needs and concerns. Maher has become skilled with creative solutions to intractable problems: creative options appear from this deep listening. Maher is also prepared to work slowly, so the changes become embedded and not lost over time, as opposed to "helicoptering in" with a pre-determined package of solutions. You already read the example of the beggars' colony and how slowly, over many years, they worked to build trust and prepare both the children and the adults before bringing some of the children to Maher for even a taste of schooling.

Travelers who come to India to Maher to volunteer learn "we see how it is; then we do the needful." firsthand. For example, this author first went to Maher at Sister Lucy's request to write a book outlining how to replicate Maher. When I arrived my first week (or more) was spent traveling around with staff seeing how Maher works, visiting a vast array of different projects, Homes and programs all over Pune District. Three other Westerners (from the U.S. and Europe) travelled with us. We did no work; we simply observed how it is. After this we split up; they began activities with children and I went off to shadow Sister Lucy. We gathered in the evenings for dinner, often with Sister Lucy and other staff where we traded stories, asked questions and learned more. I could not help but feel profound respect for Sister Lucy, the staff, the people and from such a foundation, love grows easily. It is a unique way of making use of volunteer resources; often we from the West think we know so much and know how to do certain things. It is humbling to simply listen first, and absorb and respectfully blend in. Experience teaches much more effectively than words.

Yet another way Maher grows these values in the children is the tradition of "Seva (service) Days" for their youth. In the photo below a 10th standard girl is shown helping at a home for elderly women and women with mental disabilities. This connects the generations and helps give the youth a sense of purpose in honoring their elders.

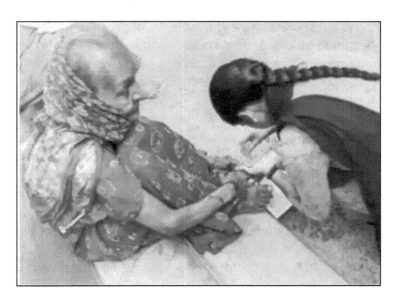

Social justice for all regardless of caste, class, or gender

This value can show up in many ways, often challenging cultural norms. For example: girl-children are often not educated, or at most only to fifth standard. Wives go live with their husband's family, raising children and waiting on their in-laws. Maher educates all children to the maximum of their ability and interest. Girls are encouraged to take leadership opportunities as they grow up in Maher, such as emceeing at large public events, entering speech contests, and more. They are encouraged to attend college and even University so they can have a professional career if interested.

Widowed women have come to Maher with their children, put out by their in-laws who could not afford to feed them, or simply believed in the tradition that widows should not re-marry. It was socially acceptable to allow the widow and children to starve. Maher worked hard to change the Indian cultural norm that a widow cannot re-marry. Now re-marriage is an accepted practice in and around communities where Maher is established.[13]

Women can come to Maher for shelter and support regardless of class. Even women from wealthy families can be abused. Poverty is not the only factor in admissions. Women, children and men on the streets, gravely ill, are picked up, cleaned, and given food and medical care. Sometimes these people have not bathed in months or have festering wounds and the smell is horrible. But Maher helps all – unconditional love and social justice in action.

Maher has also helped poor people, illiterate people, migrants, and tribals understand their legal rights due and to fight for them. Recall the case of Thakarvasti tribal area that Maher introduced to literacy, rights, capital for growth, getting

---

[13] See Rising to New Life. There are several stories of widows whom Maher has helped to remarry, including the first one in Vadhu years ago. These stories show how the culture of these villages changed over time.

the government to recognize them and build roads in, etc. The same was done for the tribals in Jharkhand. For both these communities, with Maher's assistance, the first generation of children attended school.

Truth, transparency, and fairness in all interactions and in distribution of resources

Bribes are very common in India for doing business especially with government jobs. When Sister Lucy began, she struggled for every rupee to feed and house the people she was helping. She was determined not to waste a single precious rupee paying a bribe to some official for him to do his job. She has tried waiting them out, pretending she did not understand. Then once that did not work, she pestered and pled with them. One time she invited the inspectors to come to Maher. They had been withholding her operating license for over a year. They thought that now she would finally pay them. She said yes, but you walk around with me and see the work here. At the end of the tour she said "You tell me which women and which children I must put out from Maher to pay you." They did not know what to do. They left. In a few days her license arrived. Even now, several of the Homes are waiting for license renewals, sometimes for a bribe, sometimes due to politics. But Lucy does not worry too much anymore because the Child Welfare Committee, police, local leaders and even business companies all support Maher and its vital role in the community. There would be significant protest, both locally and internationally, if Maher were shut down by the government.

Maher keeps meticulous records, accounting for every donation received and how all funds are spent. She herself takes no salary; even her clothing is donated to her. Sister Lucy shares a room with Sister Meena, one of the other nuns who has come to join Sister Lucy's work at Maher. Everyone's accommodations are equivalent, for all staff. Everyone lives simply. Everyone eats the same foods, regardless of role, caste, etc. (Exceptions are made for medical or religious requirements.)

Most meals are vegetarian; occasionally everyone will get an egg. Sometimes, as a rare treat, a local donor will bring chicken for everyone. One lovely tradition is that a local donor having a birthday comes to Maher with their friends and family to celebrate – and they bring the celebration. For example: they bring cake and ice cream for all the children and residents. The children sing the local equivalent of Happy Birthday. It is great fun for all!

Staff, volunteers and guests are not allowed to show favoritism to any child or resident with gifts or cash. For example, this author went to a local shop and bought bags of candies to have 400 or more individually wrapped pieces. Then after a big program each child and staff would get one as they filed out. (This is at Vadhu where there are about eight Homes plus nearby Rising Star Home for teen boys who all come together for programs. Sometimes children from Pune are bused in too!)

*Reawakening our personal relationship with Mother Earth
and treating her as the Body of the Divine*

This value too is quite new in India. It has always perplexed this author how Hindu people could revere the Ganga River as holy, and then throw their trash in it. The Ganga is now horribly polluted soon after it leaves its high glacier origin. Cows are also holy. They wander freely, eating trash along the roadsides, most of which is in plastic bags. The bags tangle in their stomachs and they die horrible painful deaths. But slowly this is beginning to change across India. Maher too is part of this shift in awareness. Even this author has seen a significant reduction in roadside waste in the villages near Vadhu and nearby in the last 10 years. Also actual toilets are becoming the norm instead of going outside in fields and roadsides.

Beyond trash, Maher relies heavily on solar water heating. Rooftop systems are on nearly every Maher Home, and now in the villages too. Maher has a host of related programs in its Patchwork Quilt of Services listed earlier (vermiculture pits/composting, kitchen gardens, biogas production, etc.). Solar power is being explored, though this needs further sponsors.

Lifelong learning and continual reevaluation and change

As noted earlier, Sister Lucy quickly came to see illiteracy and limited education as roots of poverty, violence and other issues. Educational opportunities are central to all Maher programs. Basic numbers and letters are taught to the self-help group participants. Adults can choose to pursue high school equivalency and either vocational or higher education if they are able and interested. All the children attend school at least through high school, and then onto community colleges, technical programs or university per their interests and abilities. In India, government schools, while very inexpensive to attend still require uniforms and book bags which can be prohibitive for poor families. These schools offer only the most basic education. Only the bare bones of English, mostly vocabulary, is taught. Children do not graduate able to speak English or even with any marketable skills. Yet community colleges and universities are taught exclusively in English, which presents a significant barrier to children who have attended the government schools. Professional level business is mostly conducted in English.

The best schools therefore are the private English-medium schools where all instruction is in English. These schools are private, expensive, and traditionally only open to upper caste Indians. Additionally, children must start here in kindergarten or they will not be able to catch up. Maher shifts small children to Homes in Pune (or other locations) where the English-medium schools are present where possible, especially if the child shows promise. This is true even when the mother and/or siblings remain in the village-based Maher Homes. Sundays, holidays and vacations are family visiting days. Maher has built relationships with several good English-medium schools in Pune and can often get at least partial scholarships for Maher children. It is a big expense, but investing in very young children has the biggest impact on their lives. Maher's youth benefit from the plentiful foreign guests at Maher. English is generally the common language, so the youths get lots of practice. This has helped many do well in college and beyond, even without attending English-medium schools as have most of their college-going peers.

Older girls and boys are encouraged to pursue higher education and vocations rather than marrying young. Indian families have the habit to marry girls very young, and so Maher works with the families to help them see the value of waiting until the girl is fully educated and can work outside the home. Then they can get married. This way not only do the girls have more self-confidence, they are also more respected by the men, and less likely to become victims of violence. Additionally, if something happens to their husband, they are able to work to support their family.

Maher had to get creative to support this higher education for young people. According to Indian law, children must be put out of children's homes at age 18, even if they are in the middle of a school year. Sister Lucy saw that if she did that, these young people would flounder and likely end up doing menial work and never rise out of poverty. So, she hired these young people and shifted them to the "adult" category and supported their continued education and development. They would work a few hours a week, for example helping tutor children, doing office work, coaching sports, etc. The money they earned they could spend on personal items or bus fare to school, for example, and so they began to learn money management as well.

Young people and staff are also exposed to special trainings, such as non-violent conflict resolution workshops. These are often sponsored by local companies. Another program that many youth and adults from Maher have now participated in is "Gender Reconciliation." This international program is unique in that men and women come together in a process to share and heal gender-based wounds and trauma. A few of Maher's young adults have even trained as facilitators in this important, leading-edge work.[14]

Sister Lucy is continually reflecting on her work at Maher – what worked well, what did not work well, what can be improved. She leads in-service days both for housemothers, and for social workers and other staff where they not only discuss upcoming plans at Maher, but also current issues and challenges, and ways the staff can improve how they work. Generally, reflection and skill trainings are part of this. Everyone at Maher, including residents, are expected to learn from their interactions and experiences and grow as human beings. Non-denominational prayer and meditation are part of this process. In fact, all the adults and teenagers attend one-day, then three-day, then 10-day Vipassana Meditation retreats at Maher's expense. Meditation on breath is a part of daily life for all Maher staff and residents as a core skill to support healing from trauma and personal reflection and development.

In the month of June, Maher brings all the housemothers together for a retreat for four days. (This is during school vacation so many children have gone home to visit parents or relatives.) The women discuss how to work with the children, how to handle difficult behavior, the best foods to provide for health, fire safety and more. Sister Lucy also makes sure she provides time for them to express all their feelings –

---

[14] Satyana Institute is a U.S.-based NGO and creator of "Gender Reconciliation" programs, offered world-wide. For more information see www.satyana.org.

frustrations, limitations, queries etc., to make sure Maher is providing a safe space for them to be heard and supported. They hold smaller trainings throughout the year, as well as times for relaxation and rejuvenation.

The Heart of Maher

These seven core values, including their operational implications and expenses, are at the heart of both Maher's uniqueness and success. They are counter-cultural in India and many do not understand at first why Sister Lucy is so committed to them in practice. But these values are responsible for the unique "feel" that is Maher: joy, love, generosity of spirit – in a community where essentially all the residents, and some staff, have experienced poverty, trauma, and more.

Many of the awareness programs held as part of the Patchwork Quilt reflect these values, such as educating girl-children, why interfaith, why caste-free, cleanliness and hygiene of villages and homes, and more. In fact, these awareness programs are a key vehicle for slowly seeding these values into daily life in the regions where Maher operates.

Even Maher's Ekta program (provisions for poor families to keep them together) is based on respect for the family. Many other organizations (in India and the West) judge the families unworthy to raise their children and take them.

So many of India's lower castes, poor, and minorities are denied education and training and so never able to rise above their birth status. Maher embraces and respects all; meeting not only basic needs for food and shelter but encouraging these people to dream of a better future for themselves and for their children. They receive the tools from Maher: education, training, encouragement, and most of all love. Hence Maher's motto of *"rising to new life."*

4: EXPANSION BEYOND PUNE DISTRICT:
Three Early Cases

Expanding beyond Pune was never part of Sister Lucy's original vision. But Maher soon began getting requests to either take over projects started by others (such as in Kerala, Ratnagiri and Miraj) or to establish new Maher centers in different parts of India (such as in Jharkhand, Kolkata, Karnataka and Bihar). As Maher's reputation grew, often land or a building was donated, or significant support was pledged in order for Maher to move forward. (such as in Karnataka and Satara). Regardless of where a new site is located, other core Maher projects such as Homes for mentally disturbed or destitute women or men were gradually added, and the programs from Maher's patchwork quilt were gradually added as well, such as village awareness raising, production, self-help groups, etc.

Three early ventures beyond Pune were all in response to pleas for help and all were rich learning grounds for all future growth. The first two were both requests to take over existing projects for orphan children run by other organizations. The third was an entirely new operation. For all three, new or additional staff had to be hired and trained. Methods of operation had to be established to match Maher's ways, requiring significant revisions in the pre-existing organizations. Maher had to build new relationships with neighbors, police, government offices such as the Child Welfare Committee, and more. There were language and travel distance challenges as well.

Regardless of where in India these new Centers were, all Maher core values and unique operating methods had to be followed. Each start-up brought unique challenges and lessons. These in turn influenced how future growth for Maher has been managed.

This chapter will tell the stories of these first three new sites. The following Chapter will summarize the challenges of growth beyond Pune, and how Maher has addressed these.

KERALA

In response to the great tsunami of 2004, a Swami in Kerala used a corner of the land of his ashram to open a small home for boys orphaned by the tragedy. Soon he realized that he and his people did not know much about raising children and began to seek alternatives. Serendipitously, Sister Lucy was from Kerala (and still has a large family there), so the Swami had heard of the nun running children's homes in Pune. He asked to meet her, and the details were worked out. The Home was separate from the rest of the ashram, so they could each continue their work without disruption.

For the first several years, this Home had its own Board of Trustees, of which the Swami was one; it was not governed by Maher's Trustees. This arrangement sometimes made it challenging for Sister Lucy to operate as she would at Maher. There were times when goals, values or methods differed. Eventually the Kerala Home and land was brought fully into Maher. Through this experience, Sister Lucy learned that Maher needed to be fully in control of any Project she ran.

Another challenge was that Kerala is at the most southern tip of India, 24-30 hours by train from Pune. Plus, Malayalam, the state language and its alphabet, are totally different from Maharashtra. Sister Lucy could speak the language since she grew up here, but in those days none of the other Maher staff could. At least Lucy enjoyed being near her parents and siblings to see them more regularly.

Because of the language barrier, no one from Pune could be sent down to run this Home or train staff. Sister Lucy had to hire new staff, selecting people who felt an affinity for Maher's values, and then train them herself in the Maher ways. Since this Home was for boys, she hired a Housefather; with luck, his wife was a nurse and also agreed to work for Maher. The Home-in-charge and social worker were also men. Mr. Vijayan, the Home-in-charge was active in the local Ghandi society, and so already shared many of Maher's core values.

A fun story about languages from this author: the cook was from Nepal – a blessing I discovered my first morning there. I went to the kitchen seeking hot milk to make my own tea (no caffeine) and I had already forgotten the (local) Malayalam words Lucy had taught me the night before. After a bit of waving arms, pointing, showing my cup, none of which was working, I finally tried asking in Hindi which I had learned a bit of years before. Serendipitously that is what the cook spoke at home in Nepal. I got my hot milk and we both had a good laugh. The many different languages in India is a challenge indeed.

On this same visit there was a small three-year-old girl child in residence. Sister Lucy explained that she and her two brothers were left here by their father, an alcoholic with no work. Their mother was dead. Maher was not allowed to have any girls here – any home for them needed to be separated from the boys by a wall, regardless of age. (Laws vary state to state.) Sister Lucy could not bear to think what would happen to this girl child if Maher did not take her in with her brothers. She was so small they dressed her in boy's clothes and tried to avoid detection. Sister Lucy was already seeking financing to build a Home for women and girls across the field. They had acquired the land and even started part of the wall. She vowed she would never again agree to a home for only boys, where families would need to be split up, especially given that girls are so much more vulnerable.

Soon the new Home was built. By this time Mini, a cousin of Sister Lucy's from Kerala, had been working in Pune overseeing the main large Vadhu site. She of course could speak Malayalam and knew Maher's ways. So she was sent down for about a year to run this new Home and train local staff. This has become a primary way that Maher values are transferred to new sites: seasoned Maher staff are transferred to lead new sites and train staff. In this way hiring and training is no longer solely up to Sister Lucy.

RATNAGIRI

The Jesuits had been operating a Home for orphan girls in Ratnagiri, a few hours south of Mumbai by train. They came to know of Maher and Sister Lucy and asked her to take over the running of this Home. They had to agree to her Interfaith operations. No bibles would be handed out, though the Bible is one of four books on every Maher altar. (The other three are the Koran, the Bhagavad Gita, and the Dhammapada.) They also had to agree that major religious (and non-religious) holidays would all be celebrated, such as Eid, Diwali,

International Women's Day, and more. Travel from Pune was not easy, traversing mountains, taking about eight hours by jeep or 12 plus hours by bus. At least however the language here was still Marathi, the same as Pune. Maher agreed to take over the management of this Home in 2009.

At first there were only girls here. Maher sent staff from Pune to help take over the operation of this Home. Soon a woman with two children came seeking shelter. They took her in with her children and trained her as a housemother, as was the practice in Pune. Pune staff could return home, only leaving a Maher social worker as In-charge with the housemother and a housemother-cook who was later hired.

The first time this author visited Ratnagiri, I experienced a Maher tradition called "exposure visits." Sister Lucy wanted the (mostly) orphaned children to see more than just a Maher building and their school. She wanted them to see something of the city and other typical sights. Ratnagiri happens to be near the coast on the Arabian Sea. Sister Lucy grew up on the coast (in Kerala) and loves the water. She wanted to give these children a chance to see the sea. So we gathered the children with some basic supplies (like bottled water). We assigned "buddy pairs": one adult or teenager with one child. We walked to the roadside bus stop and waited, nearly 30 of us! We managed to pile on. The rest of the bus riders were amazed and made space for us. I held tightly to my partner's hand: a sweet shy seven-year-old girl. We got off and walked along a pathway to a beach access. We arrived to a view of a white sandy beach and wide open soft blue sea. The children were so awed and excited. (Me too!) They played in the sand. Few were willing to venture into the water past their toes. And they ran from the waves, squealing in excited fear. A few were interested in trying to swim. In India people swim in full clothing (long tunic tops with baggy trousers). So Sister Lucy, I, and a few others waded in and demonstrated. We helped any who wanted to try. We had so much fun! We air-dried in our clothes, and then walked our sandy bodies back to the bus stop and traveled home.

This author and the other Westerner offered to pay for dinner out at a local restaurant, another first for the children. Everyone cleaned up and put on their best clothes. They dressed us westerners in borrow saris. We walked to the nearby restaurant in our buddy-pairs. We were seated at two long tables outside in the courtyard. For most, this was the first time they had ever sat at a table to eat! (Meals are traditionally taken seated on the floor.) At first the staff were nervous having 20 orphans all dining. But very quickly they were charmed and impressed by the children and their good manners. All enjoyed this fun day. The children were very tired but very happy.

My next visit to Ratnagiri was when Lucy and Hira went down for a surprise inspection. This is another Maher regular occurrence. Once or twice a year, senior staff go to each remote site and inspect all the record books, the children's lockers, bedrolls, book bags, everything about the running of the Home to be sure all processes are followed correctly. I was writing my first book about replicating Maher, so witnessing this process was invaluable. For example, going through the book bags we found a couple Christian children's books. We had to remove these. Hira explained that if the teachers or a parent found these, Maher could get in trouble for trying to convert the children. We also noted which book bags needed repairing or replacing. The children were all present for this, watching, and the older ones helped with repairs.

Another example was going through the clothing. Each child had a "locker" (here, a shiny metal trunk). Each child was required to have two clean school uniforms, two clean neat outfits, one set of "play clothes." These "play clothes" were often grubbier, but perfect for playing outside in the yard next to the Home. At this site, the dirt is red-staining and so hard it felt like lava, which was hard on fabric. We were looking for stains, tears, etc. in the clothing. Hira made a list of what was needed for each child. Then later the fun began. There was a big stash of donated clothing. The girls would come into the office in small groups based on size and we would find replacement outfits as needed. Just like any girl, trying on new-to-them clothes was fun. We learned who liked what colors and tried to satisfy all. The housemothers are supposed to keep up with this, but with 20 children it is easy to miss things. The older girls were expected to wash their own clothes, so their habits were getting inspected as well.

Lucy and Hira are both much beloved. On each of these inspections, Lucy or Hira meet one-on-one with each resident to see how they are doing and what their interests are as they are growing up. They ask if they have any complaints or issues with the local staff. They listen to woes or issues with parents or family for those children who have family. In this way too, Lucy and Hira truly come to know every child of Maher, regardless of location, i.e. literally hundreds of children.

As Maher's reputation and regard grew in this area, people began asking Maher to help more people. AIDS was a big issue in this area, but healthcare was only available for adults with AIDS. Children whose parents had AIDs or had AIDS themselves were simply put out on the streets as people were afraid to help them. Of course, there were destitute women and others in need as well.

About this time there was a change in leadership within the Jesuits and they planned to take back the house. Maher and the girls there (over 20) would have to leave. Sister Lucy began urgently looking for more land to purchase so Maher could both continue to support the girls and also meet these other needs. Finally, a family was selling a large house where there was open land on the same street. A school was close enough for the children to attend.

This author recalls walking through the family home as Sister Lucy considered how it could be remodeled to fit Maher's needs and whether to purchase it. With now over 12 years of experience Sister Lucy could quickly assess the well, sewage issues, how rooms could be re-purposed, etc. She could "see" this new Maher home! Maher signed the papers to buy the home, and some land on the same street. She knew with whom to contract for designs, building, contractors, etc. Ultimately two additional homes were built on the adjacent land, one for boys and one for AIDs-affected children. (Girl's and boy's homes must have walls with gates separating them, and any home for AIDs children needed to be separate as well.) This AIDs home is the only such home Maher operates. It was wonderful to return several years later and stay as a guest in the re-purposed home, where the older, at-risk, and mentally disturbed women now live.

Ultimately the Jesuits agreed to continue to support Maher's Home for the girls. However, this further reinforced her determination to not run Projects that Maher did not fully control and own the building and land. This is true whether the building is on loan or on rent, where a landlord can simply decide to stop renting to Maher, putting the residents at risk. This is one reason Maher tries to own the buildings in which they invest (since even most rentals need remodeling to suit so many residents). Owning is much more stable. Even with the high cost of land and building materials, it still pays off in the long run. Westerners are often shocked at the prices for land and building materials, which rival prices in the West. Land is at a premium in India with its vast population, and construction materials like rebar are bought on the world market. This is one reason so many Indians live in shacks, slums and on the streets.

When this author first visited Ratnagiri, Meera was the social worker and House-in-charge. She had come to Maher as a single mother with her small son. Her family refused to have anything to do with her. She completed her education, earned her MSW, and was fully integrated in Maher ways and values. Later when Meera's son was school age, he could no longer live in the girls Home. The boy was bright and Lucy wanted him to attend an English-medium school. So she brought them both back to Pune and sent a different Maher social worker to Ratnagiri. I later reconnected with Meera in Jharkhand when she was there for a couple of years, though her son was still attending an English-medium school in Pune. We met again when she was back in Pune supervising a Maher experimental "group home" where mentally disturbed women live in the community while working simple jobs. This is a good example how Sister Lucy deploys experienced staff to different Maher centers. By this time Meera's family had reconciled with her and I met her brother also.[15] I enjoy these small friendships across time and space and a big Maher family!

JHARKHAND

The next major expansion after Kerala and Ratnagiri was into the state of Jharkhand to the northeast, the poorest state in India. Nearly a third of the population of Jharkhand is tribal, many in remote forested regions totally avoided by the government. Many different languages are spoken in Jharkhand, though the official language is Hindi, which at least shares an alphabet with Marathi (the official language of Maharashtra state and Pune). Ranchi is the capital of Jharkhand and that is where Maher was invited. Jharkhand is about 24-30 hours by train from Pune, and there is one daily flight from Pune to Delhi then Delhi to Ranchi; either way, it is at least a full day of travel each direction. (Jharkhand is in literally the opposite direction of Kerala.)

It took persistent persuasion to bring Sister Lucy so far away when Maher was still so young (2007). Below is the story pieced together from conversations with Sister Lucy, Hira and from this author's visit.

---

[15] When these women become successful professionals, they bring respect for the whole family which facilitates reconciliations. Many families fear either the shame of an unwed mother, which could negatively affect siblings' marriage chances, and/or the potential financial drain of another set of dependents.

A firm friendship begins: Shoba's story

This story begins back at Hope House, before Sister Lucy even dreamed of Maher. (Hope House was a small convent-owned enclosure offering day programs to impoverished locals.) Sister Lucy and Shoba met here as young women working and living on site with Sister Noelene. Both sought to work at Hope House to help the people. When Sister Lucy went outside Hope House to work with the people, Shoba often went with her. Or if Sister Lucy went out and was late returning, Shoba saved her tea, food, whatever Lucy missed. They became good friends.

One day, two Brothers came to Hope House to also do some work. One of the Brothers, John, and Shoba fell in love. They were afraid to tell anyone. Shoba told Sister Lucy that they wanted to marry. Sister Lucy counseled them both to be sure they wanted to marry, knowing the hardships they would face being from different states and castes. Sister Lucy told Sister Noelene and smoothed things over so Shoba and John could marry. John had to leave the Brotherhood to get married.

Shoba came from a big, well-known Catholic family from Maharashtra. John was a tribal from Jharkhand and so of a lower caste. Because of this, Shoba's family was against the marriage. Getting married to a person from another state and caste was not very common and both the communities reacted strongly to this decision. No one from her family came for the wedding.

Sister Lucy stood by their decision as they deeply loved each other, and she arranged the marriage. Another

103

challenge was that no one had money for a wedding. Sister Lucy was often going here and there working, doing small jobs where she would earn pocket money. She saved this and used it to pay for a small, simple ceremony and they got married. Because they had no money, Sister Lucy helped find some people who could give the new couple a few things to help them start their new life together. After one or two years, Shoba and John moved to Jharkhand.

Later, Shoba's family all came around and now are very happy with her marriage to John. Once Shoba began working for Maher, her family became very proud of her and supportive of Maher. Both her parents and her brother have visited her and John in Jharkhand.

Sister Lucy remained working with Sister Noelene. Then Sister Lucy encountered the woman who came to her for help and then was burned alive by her husband. This is the incident that so deeply inspired and committed Sister Lucy to do more for these at-risk women, leading her to create Maher in 1997.

Keeping in touch: a persistent friend

The two friends kept in touch through letters and Shoba learned Sister Lucy began Maher. Over the next ten or so years, Shoba and John came to Pune for Christmas holidays to see family and Sister Lucy. They came to know of Maher and Sister Lucy's work.

Shoba was very moved by the work; each time she visited Sister Lucy at Maher, she was in tears. Shoba became committed to bringing Sister Lucy and Maher to Jharkhand. Sister Lucy told her she had a lot of work to do in Pune and rejected her invitations, but Shoba was very determined to get Sister Lucy to Jharkhand. She kept phoning.

Shoba begged Sister Lucy to come to Jharkhand and open a Maher. "Jharkhand is the poorest state in India. Please come and see the poverty there! We must help. You must come!" She kept telling Sister Lucy to not start more in Maharashtra, and instead telling her to start a Maher in Jharkhand. Shoba kept insisting, and so Sister Lucy finally agreed to visit.

The first visits

In 2007 Sister Lucy travelled to Jharkhand along with Anuradha Karkare, then President of Maher Trustees. Shoba took them around to "see how it is" in Ranchi where she and John lived.

The first home Shoba took Sister Lucy and Anuradha was the home of one family. The room was dark with no proper ventilation or electricity. They could barely see what was inside. Suddenly Sister Lucy saw a little baby wrapped in a cloth, in a cradle made of cloth. The baby was asleep all by herself in the dark room. Her mother was so thin and famished. Just then the father returned with his cycle rickshaw. He too looked very thin and miserable. While talking to the family she came to know the couple had eleven children and the father was suffering from tuberculosis. Sister Lucy realized they needed food. She told a shop keeper nearby to provide food grains, milk and whatever they needed, and Maher would pay their bill.

Shoba also took Sister Lucy and Anuradha to visit several villages around Ranchi, where they spoke to people and came to know the situation of the residents. They could see the urgent need to start the mission of Maher in Ranchi.

Later that year, Sister Lucy and Hira travelled to Jharkhand to visit Shoba and John. They again saw how bad the conditions were for the people. Shoba promised "you start it and I will help." Maher agreed that they had to do something to help. At this time, Shoba and John were renting a room from Neera, living with her in her home. From Shoba and then from these visits, Neera too became inspired by Sister Lucy and Maher. She too declared she wanted to help run the new Maher in Ranchi.

They quickly found a house to rent for the first Maher Home in Ranchi. Next both Shoba and Neera travelled to Pune for several weeks to live at Vadhu and "see how it is" and to learn Maher's ways.

October 2008 Maher inaugurated the first Home in Ranchi

Shoba and Neera returned to Jharkhand along with Hira, Zumbar (an experienced housemother) and Sandeep (an experienced male social worker). Four mentally disturbed women also came with them to live in the new house. (While the first home here was for children, they planned to quickly open a home for women as the need was great.) They all travelled on the train, bringing many of the supplies they needed since it was hard to get such items in Jharkhand: stainless steel vessels for cooking and eating, bedding, etc. Hira also had cash: about 10,000 rupees plus a check for 50,000 rupees. It is a very, very long journey (over thirty hours), plus they had the women to care for, and at some point, Hira fell asleep. She got robbed.

Hira phoned Sister Lucy right away and told her what happened. Immediately in the morning Sister Lucy called the bank to block the check. However, this still left the start-up team with no cash in hand. Shoba told John what happened and he immediately donated 50,000 rupees! (This is a lot of money for a simple working family.) This allowed the group to immediately start the work.

Hira recalls those early days

We started visiting the local families who had come to know about Maher and were waiting for us. Shoba had set this up. Those first two days we took six admissions of children. We explained everything and the parents signed the forms. This meant their children could attend school, so their parents were very happy. These were all local poor families who wanted their children to be educated so they would have a better life than their parents. And so we began.

School registration requires birth dates, parental information, and details. These children had no identification, no birth certificates, nothing. (This is common among poor people – they cannot afford the fees to pay to register the births of their children.) We had to write in a birthdate even though we did not know what it was.

We had to visit the schools and talk to the teachers. We finally found a local school willing to take these children in October, half-way through the school year. (Many schools will not take children mid-year.) We were so grateful. I walked with the children every morning to take them to school. Then Sandeep went and walked them home after school. It was nearly two or three kilometers each way and we had no vehicle.

Sandeep, Zumbar and I were there for six weeks or more. Quickly there were twenty children living in the Home. We showed Shoba and Neera how to do everything: how to work with the children, cooking, cleaning, proper hygiene, how to handle problems as they arose, etc. We showed them how to keep the accounts, the registers, timetables (schedules) for each day, programs for the children, everything. We have to keep very careful records for the government. Every tiny detail for each child has to be recorded in the right paper notebook; computer records are not accepted by the government. (These registers or notebooks include new admissions, daily school attendance, who ate what every day, how every penny was spent, how much milk each child drank daily, how many items of which pieces of clothing each child had, and more.) The government does not help fund the work, but they must approve every admission and oversee our operations and all the ways we do things.

Once things were running well, Sandeep, Zumbar and I returned to Pune.

Shoba and Neera learned to do everything very well. Shoba became House-in-charge and Women-in-charge; Neera became Children-in-charge and also responsible for the administrative work. (These are primary roles at all Maher sites.) Shoba is also a very good public relations person for Maher. We are also very grateful to her husband John: he keeps supporting his wife to do this work. Shoba lives with her husband and their children. Every morning she gets up very early, cooks and leaves food for him and their children. Then she comes to Maher to help prepare the children for school. She is at Maher until late in the evening too. He is supporting her very well and also their own children, while she works with the Maher women and children.

Both John and Shoba feel so good doing something to give to the people, and Shoba is working from the heart. They very much wanted to help the people, and now they can.

Maher Pune staff is always on call: Vagisha's story
Sister Lucy told this story.

"Vagisha was a Catholic tribal woman. She came to us soon after we started the Children's Home in Jharkhand. She told us she was suffering from domestic violence. She said she needed immediate shelter. At that time, we had started the home only for children and had only the license for children; we had not started officially taking in women. But Vagisha said she needed immediate shelter. Jharkhand staff phoned me and asked what shall we do?

"Of course I said take her in and let her stay in the children's home because she had two children with her (two boys, aged eight and four). She had fled her home with her two children. So I said keep them all with the children, her children along with our children. Let it be.

"Soon we gave her a job as a housemother. Her two children began to attend school and get a good education. But somehow her husband came to know where they were. When he was drunk, he used to come to the Maher home to harass her. Then we had to close the doors and windows so he did not upset her. Once he broke all our windows and then we had to pay to replace all of them. Next time he came he broke the door to get inside, to get to her. She did not want to go with him. She said to him "how can I go with you when you are so violent?" We had to call the police to get him away. Things like that happened, on and off.

"The staff were really scared; they feared he might even harm not only his family but other of Maher's children. Once he even did this: one child (not his own) went up to him to tell him not to hurt the woman, so he hit that child.

"So now what to do? By now we had opened the first Home out in the villages. We shifted Vagisha from the house in Ranchi to the new Maher house out in the villages in Jharkhand. But somehow he managed to find out where she went. He went there and beat her up.

"Again, I wondered what to do? Staff knew that if we sent her back home, both her life and the two children's lives would be in danger. But they rightly feared for the staff and other residents of Maher. They said "we do not know what to do with her. You must tell us."

"What to do with her? Or with him? I sent Hira and Sandeep back to Jharkhand. They got there and analyzed the full situation. They told me this man is giving so much trouble and it is going to be very dangerous to keep the woman here. He will come for her all the time.

"I could not simply bring them all to Pune. I wanted the children to be able to continue their education, but they know only Hindi and so they would have to learn Marathi to even go to school in Pune, let alone communicate with other children and housemothers. And I did not want to bring only the mother to Maher Pune because I did not want the children to be separated from their mother too, since they were already separated from their father. And even if we brought the mother to Pune, the children might still be at risk from the father if they remained in Jharkhand. It looked hopeless.

"So what I did, I told Hira and Sandeep to bring the father to Maher Pune. When he was drunk, they managed to get him on a train to Pune. He was so dirty and so drunk he was not even aware what was happening. He was shouting and using abusive language and was an embarrassment to staff and a nuisance to people on the train. By evening, he said he needed to use the toilet, so they walked with him. He tried to jump the train to get more alcohol. Sandeep managed to prevent him from jumping; even if the train is going slow people try to jump and it is still dangerous. They got him back to the seat and like this they reached Pune nearly thirty-four hours later.

"Fortunately for him and for us, he made up his mind not to drink. He began working at Maher. On and off sometimes he goes to drink, but not all the time. He worked in the garden with John (another long-time staff member) at Vatsalydam.

"When he was alright, and the children as teenagers were old enough to understand, then I first brought the mother here to the man. She began working in the kitchen at Vatsalydam. We put them in a family room at Maher so they could live together. Both had good jobs at Maher and both were doing well.

"The children were also doing well. When the younger boy first came to us in Jharkhand, he had not yet started school, so we were able to send him to English-medium school. This meant he could transfer to a Pune English-medium school when his mother came here. Once the mother settled and we could see it was alright, then this younger boy came. The older boy was still in Jharkhand because he was in Hindi-medium school. When he completed his twelfth standard, because college will be taught in English anyhow, he too came to Pune. Now the whole family is here together."

Expanding from Ranchi: villages and tribal areas

Maher knew the needs were great outside Ranchi in the village and tribal areas as well. From the base of the Ranchi Home, Maher could begin awareness programs in the villages, just as they had done in Pune district. Here too they addressed topics such as the value of education for both boys and girls, the dangers of alcohol, hygiene, women's rights, tribal rights, and more. Relationships were built. Soon some people helped Maher acquire some land about an hour outside Ranchi. There Maher built a new "campus" including a Home for women and girls, and a separate Home for boys.[16] Next a Home for mentally disturbed women was added. In 2021 a Home for men was under construction. All of these are enclosed by a wall for security and there is some garden and play space.

Maher now has five or six Homes in two locations: in capital city of Ranchi and the larger remote site in the countryside. Shoba and Neera supervise all these sites in Jharkhand.

---

[16] In Jharkhand, legally the boys can live in the same compound if the sleeping spaces are separate from the girls', as opposed to Kerala where they had to be in totally separate walled off quarters, even for meals.

Self-help groups and the tribal areas
Sister Lucy told this story.

Another organization, (a Christian religious congregation), had trained some local para-social workers to start self-help groups (SHGs) for the people in the more remote villages and tribal areas outside Ranchi. Sister Pilar was in charge of this, but then she got ill and had to leave, so the work and support stopped. When Maher first came to Ranchi, these para-social workers came to tell us about the conditions and the work they were doing. At this point they had no support and the village people had no help or guidance any more. This was about 2008.

We met with all of them and saw the village conditions. We explained who we were, our values including interfaith, how we work etc. The women were happy to join. To begin, we brought this group of about six para-social workers to Pune for eight days to see Maher, and to learn Maher values and spirit. I wanted them to feel what life was like at Maher. Staff showed them all the different Maher projects (women, children, mentally ill, production center, kindergartens, etc.) and took them to see some of the area SHGs. They were very pleased and eager to do the work in Jharkhand as part of Maher.

SHG's in Jharkhand tribal areas: Helen's story

Maher then took job applications from this group of women to become Maher employees as para-social workers. The group needed a supervisor since Maher was so far away. (In those days, Jharkhand did not have a fulltime social worker.) Maher staff noticed that one woman of their group, Helen, had particular talent. She was also a widow, she was poor, and though she had children, she had more time than some of the other women. She was genuine and talented, so we invited her to take on the extra responsibility. She was very happy to do this.

Helen began working very well, supervising the others and sending regular reports to Maher. The number of SHGs grew. By 2019 there were about 180 SHGs in this area, involving more than 5000 women and youth. Each para-social worker had thirty or so SHGs that they supported. These were mostly in the interior villages and with tribal people in the forested areas. These people had no employable skills, no income, they did not know their rights as tribals, and they needed a lot of support.

The SHGs became a steppingstone for us to start the awareness programs out in these villages. People were told about the importance of education, especially for the girl-child, what was superstition, child marriage, health and hygiene and more. In this way, Helen's team of para-social workers became responsible for not only SHGs but village development utilizing our "Patchwork Quilt" of services. In addition to organizing awareness programs, our Pune Production staff helped Helen and her team establish skill-training classes, such as tailoring or beauty care, in many villages. This enabled the women to start businesses in their own homes and earn some money. By 2019 there had been over 150 trainings to date in these villages.

Then in about 2018 Helen got sick. When she told us, we brought her to Pune. We set things up for her to supervise the work from Pune and to receive medical care. She had cancer; we took her to doctors, got her treatment. She felt better and wanted to go back to Jharkhand and do her chemo there. Sadly, it was too late – her cancer was too advanced. She died in Jharkhand.

In those last months, Helen saw a child very sick and unable to walk. She sent photos to Maher. Maher told her to take the child to the doctor and Maher would pay whatever medical expenses were required. Now the child is walking and healthy. She was so very dedicated and worked to the very end of her life.

NOTE: This author attended a graduation celebration Maher held for women completing skill training courses in several area villages. We parked the jeep on the outskirts of one village. Many people were there to meet us. All were dressed in their best clothes. There was music and chanting as we were escorted through the village to the celebration grounds. It was a grand party with multiple villages gathering and people of all ages. Certificates were presented to all the graduates. There were games for the children. Some Maher staff had gone ahead with supplies and, together with the villagers, served a hearty meal to all.

This author later learned that this event was held in one of the "border" villages. There were still Maoist guerrillas in the deeper forested areas and villages and Sister Lucy feared taking white people in there. Maher's village campus had been harassed by these guerillas for the first couple of years; after that they left Maher alone.

The people were desperately poor

With each new SHG Maher staff practice "we see how it is" and start with where the group is. They see the people's culture, their mindset, their economic background, their problems. Only then would they start a SHG, and then only according to the hearts and minds of the people, and what they can afford. They might even start with dues of only two rupees, or five rupees, per month. But with no income at all, one cannot save anything. In these interior villages the people were desperately poor. The para-social workers had to teach the villagers how to save even just one paisa in order to save up for two or six or ten rupees for the monthly SHG dues.[17]

---

[17] Many Indians never even see such small money. A rupee is valued a bit under one penny in U.S. dollars, and a paisa is about 1/100th of a rupee.

Through the SHG meetings, the para-social workers came to know of everybody's status. In this way they came to know of a woman who was very, very poor; she did not even have a few rupees to join the local SHG. She was so desperately poor she could not feed her children. She wanted a loan of 5000 rupees to start a vegetable garden business. Maher loaned her this money directly and now she has a good business and a nice house. She paid Maher back fully.

COVID stories from Jharkhand

During the COVID-19 lockdown of 2020-21, the children of the remote Jharkhand site surprised and awed everyone – including Sister Lucy – with their ingenuity, initiative and resilience. Below are a few stories.

While Sister Lucy had some foresight and warned all the Maher centers across India to set by a month's worth of food supplies, the remote Maher site in Jharkhand was especially hard hit. Very soon this site and the surrounding area was out of electricity, water, gas cylinders for cooking, and firewood. Sister Lucy felt helpless back in Pune, under lock-down, and not even able to send help.

The children had the idea to dig a well. Sister Lucy was afraid of injury to those digging. Wells in much of India are still big round deep holes with reinforced sides that then fill up, if you hit water. It is easy to fall during the digging. Or, worse, when water rushes in, to get caught and even drown. All the work is done with hand tools and there is no safety equipment. Sister Lucy thought the risk was too great and told them no.

The children took matters into their own hands and selected the site. Usually Maher pays an engineer to find the best sites for wells where there will be water, but this was not possible. The children started digging with everyone, boys and girls, taking turns. Staff took their turns as well. The smallest children looked on.

A big, deep, round hole was dug, with smooth, tall sides. Crude hand tools were all they had. They worked for many days. Water!! The water began to flow in and everyone got out safely. They were elated of course and hurried to send news and photos to Sister Lucy. Their efforts and ultimate success were posted on FaceBook for Maher Friends worldwide to cheer. It is still mind-boggling to me (and to Sister Lucy) that they somehow knew where to dig!

One element of this story did not make it to FaceBook. For this type of well, buckets had to be lowered down by hand to dip up water. But Maher had no rope with which to lower a bucket. This challenge again required ingenuity. The children spotted a couple of empty cement bags made of woven plastic and re-wove these into a thick strong rope! Nothing is thrown out and wasted in India. They now have plenty of fresh water.

They were still however without electricity, firewood or gas. Cooking the Indian staples of rice, dal and chapatis was not possible. Each day the children went out into the bush and collected bags of leaves that they could burn to cook with.

When staff learned they would be able to get firewood at some point from Maher in Ranchi, the children again took the initiative. They approached some neighbors and asked to borrow wood and then repay it when they got theirs. The neighbors agreed. They were ultimately paid back too.

Through all this, these children and staff, far away from most "civilization" and with so very little, remained cheerful. They see their deprivations as challenges to overcome one by one. They are all working together as one big family – the Maher way.

By 2023 there were over 180 children among the Jharkhand Homes. They had been hearing about the much beloved annual "Sports Camp" that Maher holds every year in the Pune area. The children repeatedly requested to have their own Sports Camp in Jharkhand. Their wish was finally granted the summer of 2023. Maher Vadhu staff and youth traveled to Jharkhand to help facilitate the four-day event featuring various games, sports, and other competitions like acting, singing, dancing, public speaking, and more. This lively, friendly, inclusive event was a big success for the children.

5: CHALLENGES AND LESSONS LEARNED, GROWTH INTO NEW STATES

Through the three stories of the expansion of Maher's work into Kerala, Ratnagiri and Jharkhand, you have gained an idea how "the Maher way" (including values) gets communicated to sites far from Maher's home base. Over the years, Maher has grown more adept at leveraging their incredible staff and strengths to spread the Maher way. Maher now has 68 homes in seven states across India: Maharashtra, Kerala, Jharkhand, Andhra Pradesh, Karnataka, Kolkata in W. Bengal, and most recently in Bihar.[18]

Some of the common elements now to start a new center:

- invitation to bring Maher: heart-felt requests with promises of local support

- land and/or building donation, in cash or in-kind

- Maher staff goes in to "see how it is"

- experienced, senior staff go to manage start-up

---

[18] See Appendix 1 for a map showing the states of India where all these Homes are located.

- local staff are carefully selected who are pre-disposed to the Maher way

- key local staff from new site brought to Pune/Vadhu to have the lived, felt experience of life at Maher

- Maher experienced staff provide step-by-step guidance in processes, values, activities, how to work with children, families, etc. and, most importantly, how to lead by example as inevitable challenges arise

- Children receive the best possible education plus activities such as meditation, taekwondo, dance, computers, art, music, sports camps, leadership opportunities, and more

- Patchwork Quilt of services extended per local needs

Even after the seasoned Maher staff return to Pune, the local staff left behind are always part of Maher's network of support, guidance and resources. A listening ear is always available. Sister Lucy maintains a presence with phone and in-person visits. This author has visited all of Maher's sites except the newest two. Each place had the "Maher feel" of love, joy, engagement and connection to the local community, regardless how far from Pune we were.

The languages, even cultures, of all these states are different, but Maher's values, mission, and vision carry on in all of them.

CHALLENGES OF EXPANDING BEYOND MAHARASHTRA STATE

Logistics: distances, travel, language, oversight

The stories from Kerala and Jharkhand mentioned several logistics challenges: travel distances of 24 hours and more, one way, plus language barriers. Oversight is another logistical challenge. Communication regarding day-to-day management challenges, most often by phone, takes time and patience.

The Indian government oversight requires a lot of minute data, collected in separate handwritten record books. Examples include one book where daily servings of milk, per child, are recorded; another for each child's daily attendance at school; another for noting exactly what pieces of clothing each child has; another for in-kind donations; another for cash expenditures (e.g. milk, bottled gas, oil, household items, etc. which are each often separate expenditure transactions; visits from families of children and any cash or gifts left, such as a toothbrush or hair-tie; and many more. These records must be kept by hand on paper both since there is a distrust of computers by the government, and some remote centers have no access to computers or Wi-Fi, let alone secure rooms with climate control to protect the equipment. Each center must submit copies to both their local government and to Maher for centralizing record-keeping, sometimes via mail, sometimes being hand-delivered to Pune if someone from staff is going that way. As at Ratnagiri, Maher does surprise inspections of all these registers once or twice a year, to assure all is correctly entered and up to date.

One might think this is inefficient on Maher's part – why not just a few large, centralized centers to make this easier? Maher is organized for the well-being of children. Children thrive living in as close to a home and family environment as possible where each child is seen, known and supported as their own unique individual self. This is not possible in large institutions. Maher Homes are generally 20-25 children maximum, with two housemothers to lovingly focus solely on those children and their developmental needs, with social worker support.

Maher also learned quicky how to use these distances to advantage, such as shifting the violent husband from Jharkhand to Pune. Sometimes the women may be shifted, depending on the situation.

Laws vary state to state

While Child Welfare Committee operates in all states of India, the actual regulations vary by state. For example, in Maharashtra girls and boys may live in the same building until the age of six. This is helpful when a woman flees with very young children: they do not need to be separated. But in Kerala state girls and boys may not be in the same building regardless of age, putting Maher at risk when Sister Lucy chose to keep the three-year-old girl with her brothers, rather than refusing her admittance. This situation created great urgency to get the home for women and girls completed. Sometimes disabled men and disabled women can be in the same compound if each has a separate building; sometimes these homes have to be separated by a wall and gate. Maher needs to know the nuances of all the laws and regulations in each of the seven states where Maher now operates.

Seeding these values across different states,
languages and distances

Each time Maher opens a new center beyond Pune District new staff and residents must be exposed to Maher's values, and gently coached to live and relate in new ways. As with the areas around Pune, neighbors, government agencies, and more will also be exposed and slowly be influenced. Again, these values are counter-cultural for most of Indian people. While staff can be brought to Pune for several weeks to get the feel of these, residents cannot. Therefore, it is a challenge to help everyone experience and learn how to bring the values alive in daily life at every Maher Home and in every interaction. These are not simply a set of rules on a piece of paper, in fact this author does not recall seeing them written out for staff and residents in general except more recently in a staff handbook they receive upon hiring. Rather the values are lived and breathed and built into daily schedules and activities; people learn them by doing. So it would be silly to expect a new site with new staff to simply "get it." And the farther the new site is from Maher, and the more Maher grows, Sister Lucy cannot spend enough time at a new site to lead these values.

Maher quickly learned the value of sending experienced staff, such as social workers and housemothers, to open new sites. These people aren't there just for a few weeks, but months, even years. Staff know they may be asked to shift to even far away sites. Sometimes this is for start-ups as when Sister Lucy shifted Mini to Kerala, or Zumbar and Sandeep to Jharkhand. These were shorter-term. Other times the move is for maintaining values, expertise and oversight, as when she shifted Meera to Jharkhand. Meera was there a couple of years. They in turn hire and oversee local staff to help run the sites; women who come for shelter grow into housemothers or housemother-cooks to care for children as part of their healing process.[19]

Slowly over time Maher values become embedded in daily life and operations. Recently Sister Lucy has been able to send some of the cadre of young people from a generation who grew up at Maher. After completing their education, several returned to work as Maher staff in various roles. These remarkable young people, the "fruit" of Maher's work, are the best ambassadors.[20] These young adults grew up in Sister Lucy's lap and at her side; to them, the values are simply "how it is."

One such example occurred during the startup of Andhra Pradesh. Sister Lucy sent Gaus along with a seasoned housemother to get things going. Gaus came to Maher at age seven; by now he had completed his MBA and worked for a time in Human Resources at a company, then returned to Maher to work. He and a seasoned housemother had been sent here to help. Gaus was getting to know the cook and learned he was a bit worried leaving his elderly mother at home alone all day while he worked. She is healthy but has

---

[19] Women Healing Women highlights this core unique practice.

[20] See Rising to New Life chapter "Fruits of Maher" for stories of several of these young people.

nothing to do. Gaus told him to bring her here and they would find appropriate work for her to do and then they could be together (and earn a bit of extra money too). The cook was astonished and pleased. He asked how Gaus could even come up with such an idea! But this is the Maher way.

These values impact not only life inside Maher but also all Maher staff interactions with local communities, government officials, neighbors, and more. Awareness programs are begun. Long-standing cultural traditions, superstitions, gender and caste relations, and religious unrest are all gently challenged. Slowly, slowly, one relationship, one family, one village at a time begins to embrace these Maher values, of course while still practicing their own faiths.

Shifting Maher staff among locations has become an invaluable tool to spread the Maher way. This author has visited every Maher site up to 2020. All the sites indeed have the same daily rhythms and routines, the same altars and interfaith prayers, and most importantly, the same joyful, loving feel. Children are energetic and eager to engage with strangers, play games, learn yoga, or whatever is on the schedule. This is despite some combination of being orphans, having experienced trauma, separation or loss of family, illness, disability, and poverty. Each child is unique and encouraged to grow into their own unique true self.

New relationships: neighbors, police, Child Welfare Committees, and more

Each new locale meant developing new relationships with neighbors, government officials, police, etc. Maher's values and principles are radical for India – both for regular people but also for officials. Relationship building and education must start from scratch in each new location.

One example is the local office of the federal Child Welfare Committee (CWC). Every new child's admission must go through the local CWC. Whether children were found on the street or arrived with their mother, all must be officially registered and approved within 24 hours of arrival to assure a child is not being harmed or trafficked. Homes are inspected; piles of paperwork completed. These committees can cause a lot of trouble for an organization like Maher, so good working relationships are critical. In Pune, the CWC not only respects Maher, but has come to rely on them to take the difficult cases other institutions cannot manage.

This is similarly true for the local police. They can create difficulties, but once trust is established, they can be wonderful allies. In Pune, Maher is well-respected by the police. In fact, they now often bring troubled children (such as street children, beggars, even petty thieves) to Maher instead of arresting them. Police have also become allies in efforts to end domestic violence, something the police routinely ignored. Families that Maher helped reunite know that if the woman experiences trouble again, she can call Maher and even the police for support.

One case example from Rising to New Life: a troubled teen ran away from Maher's Satara site and by law Maher must report this to the police. Eventually, after being raped, she called Maher asking to come home. She was about 10-12 hours away by jeep. Maher Pune staff was closer, so they collected her, but had to bring her to the Satara Police station. Normally police retain such runaways for at least a week while they ascertain if Maher (or the NGO) abused her causing her to flee. Sister Lucy wanted this girl to be home at Maher as soon as possible to be surrounded with people she knows and who can care for her. Since Satara was a very new site for Maher, Sister Lucy asked the local police to call the Pune police to verify Maher's reputation. They did so and the girl was back at Maher in two days.

Sister Lucy has also made a point of learning who are the local leaders and she works to cultivate respectful relationships with them. She never judges anyone for their political, religious or cultural beliefs; she listens respectfully. Over time, she slowly expands their thinking and brings them around with patience and love. One example was allowing widows to remarry (a cultural taboo in most of India). Sister Lucy worked with a village leader to slowly bring him around, which helped bring around other villagers. This made life for the new couple much easier.

Creatively adapt to land and/or buildings offered but not ideal

Generous, well-intentioned supporters have given Maher buildings that have proven less than ideal for Maher's way of working. Over the years Maher has learned to use space very efficiently. Large rooms are ideal because they can become multipurpose spaces. For example, in most sites the children sleep on padded bedrolls on the floor, all in one room. (Sleeping in your own room, on a raised bed, is quite uncommon in most of India, except for the wealthy.) The bedrolls are then rolled up each morning and the room is ready for mealtime. Again, the children (and adults) sit on the floor in a circle, sing their interfaith prayers, and eat. Then this large space is cleaned and used for children to sit and do schoolwork, or games, or for the whole community to gather in a meeting. There might be a smaller room for the social worker, or for a few guests. (This author when visiting some of these Homes, has slept on the floor on one of these padded bedrolls. Not what I am used to but certainly ok.) Guest rooms will often have a simple raised cot or bed with a thin mattress to make foreign guests more comfortable. The homes for aged and mentally or physically challenged women and men have beds with mattresses too.

However when a home is donated that once housed a private family, often there are many smaller rooms. Sister Lucy and senior staff have become adept at adapting to more subdivided spaces, even moving walls when possible. Other homes have been built for Maher specifically by well-intentioned donors, but in their image of what would be a beautiful Home. One of these has a big open-air shiny stone entry area, architecturally lovely, that is nearly useless yet is close to one third the footprint of the entire building! Part of this open-air porch can be used for large public gatherings and the children can do yoga or meditation out here. There are lots of smaller rooms and wide hallways on the second floor which work for guests, but that floor is mostly empty when there are no guests. The children (even teens) cannot be spread out and away from the housemothers and staff: mischief is too tempting, especially to children who grew up in slums or on the streets.

Maher inherited other Homes when it took over a project on request. For example: a Priest had been operating a boys' home in a slum area in Miraj. When he died, the diocese begged Sister Lucy and Maher to take it over. She agreed.

You cannot drive a four-wheeler to this Home: the driver parked the Maher jeep on one edge of the slum and this author, along with Sister Lucy, Hira, Mangesh and two other foreigners trooped in. We wove through the maze of buildings and shacks to this small, small Home. We were on a 10-day "tour" to celebrate Maher Day at multiple locations around Maharashtra state. Sister Lucy described how the Home had been when she first came here two or three years prior: it was filthy and uninhabitable by Maher standards. The orphan boys were shifted to other Maher homes, where they received medical care, grooming, clean clothes and enrolled in school. Next a group of Maher staff and a couple of foreign volunteers came and scrubbed and painted. They began to get to know their neighbors in the slum. Many here are Muslim. This Home began to focus on caring for women found on the streets and/or mentally or physically challenged, perhaps traumatized, perhaps widows, or perhaps that way since birth. The families in such an area would have no resources to care for such people and so would put them out. This Home was not big enough to house both boys and girls with enough separation to meet government rules. Some very small children (under five years old) could stay here, but once they were school-aged, they would have to be shifted to another Maher Home.

Yet even here, Maher held a big celebration using an adjacent dirt track that passed as a road through the slum. A stage and loudspeakers were brought in; food was prepared. The "Chief Guests" were a local policeman, a teacher from an area school, and a local woman who taught stitching to some of the women residents. It was clear Maher already had a wonderful reputation as a partner organization serving this community. Awareness programs have already begun. This author and my fellow foreigners walked down the road before the sun set to see more of the slum. Many people had teeny houses, sometimes with a goat or chickens. Many tried very hard to keep their home neat and clean. We all smiled at each other in friendly ways, though no language was shared. A number of the children from the slum came to sit for part of the program. All who came got a yummy warm samosa, a deep-fried treat filled with potatoes, peas and spices, plus a sweet of some sort. Some of the children were Muslim, some Hindu. It was astonishing all that Maher staff managed in this tiny place!

Maher now tries to find land with buildings that can host multiple Maher projects: children (boys and girls), aged women, disturbed women, aged men, disabled men, plus a production center at least. Andhra Pradesh, Bihar, Wardha are three such new sites. It is a big up-front expenditure but saves money and headaches in the long run. Wherever Maher starts, there are always many children and people with different needs. It is naïve to assume a single house will be "enough" in any given site. Helping only one group is just not the Maher way. Therefore, Maher now tries to plan ahead by selecting and purchasing sites which can accommodate a Maher campus.

Below are some of the new Centers opened in additional states in India in the last few years.

OTHER STATES IN CHRONOLOGICAL ORDER

Kolkata

A Kolkata Home was a dream of an American supporter of Maher. Sister Lucy hesitated for many years because it is so far away, and Maher had zero contacts there. Finally Maher bought land at the request and support of these American donors. However, without an established presence here, they were unable to build a building. After several years in limbo, Maher took a house on rent nearby for mentally affected women needing shelter. Sister Lucy sent senior social worker Suprabha Alhat to lead this project. Suprabha has been with Maher for many years and is known for her infectious joy, tireless spirit, and calm wisdom. This worked for a couple of years. Then, just prior to the start of COVID, Maher took a second house on rent for mentally affected men.

Suprabha built awareness of Maher and their wonderful reputation in the surrounding communities. In addition to Homes for women and children, Maher Kolkata offers a broad range of community outreach projects including awareness programs, classes for different ages in dance, tailoring, computers and more, all drawn from Maher's Patchwork Quilt of services. Accordingly, Maher Kolkata partners with people who work at the brick kilns. Maher provides childcare and helps these children transition to attending local schools, otherwise a rarity for this community. Maher Kolkata also provides disaster relief services such as during COVID and the Cyclone of 2020. (More on Kolkata disaster relief in the next chapter.)

Of course, here Maher ran into the issues noted earlier about needing space for different groups of residents: women, men, mentally disturbed women, girls and boys, and so forth. After renting homes there for several years, they began collecting funds to build a home on the land they had already purchased but had not raised what was needed.

Serendipitously, a gentleman had built a for himself, then decided to migrate to Japan. He offered his house to Mother Teresa's Sisters. At that time, they could not manage to start another home. The Sisters of Mother Teresa were aware of Maher's work and the urgency of the need in Kolkata. They decided to offer this home to Maher. Mother General herself came for the grand opening and blessed the Home which Maher named "Maher Shubh Arambh" (Joyful Beginning). There was an issue with the original donor who expected the Home to be Catholic rather than Interfaith, but this was settled. Maher cleaned and equipped the home before moving in.

This Home, while a blessing, is not enough to replace the two rented Homes, so as of 2023 Maher is seeking funds to build another Home on the land they already purchased to replace the Homes they have on rent.

Andhra Pradesh

The site in Andhra Pradesh was the first "campus" site Maher purchased. It had originally been a retreat center and already had multiple buildings, including guest rooms, all on a large plot of land. It had been abandoned and snakes had moved in everywhere, so the price was right. Maher cleaned and restored it and it is now a thriving center.

Karnataka

The next new Homes were in Loni Bijapur in Karnataka. This land was a gift from an older gentleman. He was saddened that there were no organizations locally who were offering services to help the homeless. He became aware of Maher and reached out to request that Maher build a Home here. Maher agreed. In 2022, three new homes were inaugurated: for children, for elderly women, and a short-stay home for women. In 2024 Maher will build a Home for the men.

Bihar

The new Center in Bihar was the next example of buying a "campus" instead of starting out with a House on rent, or a single donated building. Bihar is in the far north of India, again a long way from Pune. Like Jharkhand, Bihar is a deeply impoverished part of India. The seller had heard of Maher and offered this site at a below-market rate. He knew the great needs in this area and wanted to help. Thanks to foreign donors, Maher was able to purchase this site and is currently working on renovations, even as they have begun taking in residents.

Wardha

The most recent "campus" purchase is Maher's Wardha site. This is in eastern Maharashtra (one of India's largest states), so still several hours from Pune. Maya and Atul Shelke, the social worker couple from Apti village, were promoted to be

In-charge at Wardha. Maya's 20 plus years of experience being embedded in Apti make her a perfect candidate. They moved there along with their two young daughters. Both have aging parents in this region, so this also moved the families closer together. Here too the owner knew of Maher's work and offered a below-market rate. This site is being renovated and developed for Maher use, even while they have begun to take in residents, both men and women.

Summary

These five new sites represent a lot of growth for Maher in just four years. Fortunately, Maher has a talented and committed staff that have risen to this growth, taking on the new centers and able to replicate Maher's core values and ways of working. All the Patchwork Quilt of services are deployed in all these sites as well. Surrounding villages and families are uplifted, well beyond the direct residents of these new Homes. Some of the first generation of young people who came to Maher at very young ages and grew up with Sister Lucy are now fully educated and quite a few have returned to Maher to work full time. Some of them are going out to these new sites to spread the Maher way.

6: SPECIAL SITUATIONS CALL FOR SPECIAL MEASURES

"Times of uncertainty invite us to open our minds to new possibilities" (Sister Lucy)

One of Maher's staff said on a ZOOM call to U.S. supporters that "Sister Lucy's mind is like a rocket ship! A thought comes from the universe... and WOW she manifests it!"

A U.S. supporter "chatted" back "And she does so with grace and perfection, with the support of the amazing community and team she has attracted and built and nourished. Miracle workers of LOVE made manifest."

This apt description is on full display as Sister Lucy and Maher rise to the unimaginable challenge of COVID, cyclones and more.

COVID & HUMANITY'S KITCHEN

Maher Ashram quickly deployed emergency relief services in response to COVID beginning in March 2020.

When COVID came to India, the government response was fully centralized. The Prime Minister called for an immediate and complete lockdown, with essentially no warning for people to prepare. For wealthy people in cities with food supplies, refrigeration and money, they could get by. Many white-collar workers could continue to work remotely.

But in India millions – in cities and all over the country – are household workers, drivers, day laborers, vegetable stand sellers, owners of small shops, etc. Day laborers eat on the days they have work; they go home to hovels with no food supplies let alone refrigeration. Drivers, whether of rickshaws or cabs, or "on call" for wealthy people who own cars, were immediately out of work. Often these drivers, and even household workers, sleep on the floor in the houses they serve, or have a cot in a crude basement area shared with servants of other apartments in large high rises. These drivers and household servants were fired and made to leave (out of fear of COVID). Small shops are still the most common source of food and materials for daily living. All were closed by government order, even if they sold food, so shop keepers had no income and could not even legally go to their own shop to protect what they had. Police harassed anyone on the streets.

Millions across India were suddenly jobless, homeless, afraid, and desperate. Many of these people had come to the cities in search of work to support their families. Sometimes the families came too; sometimes the worker would send money home. Therefore, these people felt they had no other option but to try to walk back home to their villages – often hundreds of kilometers away. (All public transport was shut down during lockdown.)

Soon refugees from cities, such as Pune and Mumbai, were streaming past Maher's main gates in Vadhu Budruk. They had no money or food. At first they came in the day time, but they were harassed and threatened by the police. They began to travel at night and hide during the day to avoid police.

From Maher's Facebook page*: Some are walking from Pune to Nagpur, Indore, Delhi, Madya Pradesh, and Wardha. There is not a single restaurant open, not even a tea shop. All that Maher can do is to share a warm meal. We know what we do is not even a drop in the ocean of problems they are facing.*

Migrant workers were also stranded: they were not allowed to work the fields and not allowed to be on the roads traveling. Food rotted in the fields. Families were desperate and afraid.

Meanwhile, Sister Lucy had been following international news and heard of lockdowns and fear in other countries. Just in time, she had all Maher Homes order extra food staples such as rice, wheat, lentils, cooking oil, as much as they could store. In true Maher fashion, when she saw these refugees streaming past, staff began to make huge quantities of rice and dal (traditional Indian lentils) vegetable and bread to serve warm on the streets outside Maher's gates. When the migrants began travelling at night, Maher served them late into the night.

She told of one father who walked past with three small children. They had nothing but the clothes on their backs and a small packet of cookies. This family was only one of thousands. Maher fed them all a warm meal, gave them water, blankets and food supplies. She then directed them onward to the next Maher site about 30 kilometers further along their route, where they were given another hot meal.

Well over 30,000 people were helped this way in Pune area alone. Maher named this effort "Humanity's Kitchen." Staff worried there would be no food left to feed their own residents. But Sister Lucy said "We have to give, the Divine will provide." Soon the word got out that Maher was helping these people. Donations of food and cash began arriving from local residents (even the very poor wanted to help) and local businesses. A car would show up at night and leave a bag of rice or five-gallon tin of oil. A farmer would bring bags of vegetables gleaned from his fields. Maher never ran out of food!

Finally, in May, the Maharashtra government sent buses for these travelers and stranded migrant workers to return home. Humanity's Kitchen closed.

Maher also began making up free grocery kits to distribute: nutritious staples packed in shopping bags sewn from old saris. At least 62,000 families were served this way in Pune District alone. Additionally such kits were made and distributed from Maher centers in Ratnagiri, Jharkhand, Kerala, Andhra Pradesh and Kolkata. More than 100,000 kits were distributed in all. These kits contained, for example, rice, cooking oil, soya beans, potatoes, spices, tea powder, sugar, sometimes even soap and hand sanitizers.

Maher continued to distribute these kits well into COVID, beyond the time of Humanity's Kitchen, as per the need.

Sister Lucy (center) distributing food kits to a long line of people.

*COVID spreads: Maher Ashram offers
free community programs*

As people in the villages surrounding Maher's main center in Vadhu Budruk began to sicken with COVID, they often died without receiving any medical care. The people had no way to reach the hospitals, and the hospital ambulance services were overwhelmed or were unwilling to come to the villages to collect people since most could not afford to pay. (Ambulances are not free in India, even from government hospitals. Most hospitals are private. Health insurance or an "economic safety net" does not exist in India.) Maher asked foreign donors for funds to purchase two ambulances. Maher hired drivers and posted flyers all around the area, in many villages, with a phone number to call for free ambulance service and help.

Sometimes calls received were for other kinds of help needed. For example, Maher received a call that a child needed help immediately. The caller said that the mother was in hospital, the father could not help, the three-year-old child was alone. Maher did not understand why the father could not help but sent a jeep. It turned out the father was handicapped. When Maher tried to take the child, it cried and cried. The child was afraid to leave papa and did not understand why it had to go. Maher would have taken the father too, but he wanted to stay in the house in case anything was needed for his wife. The mother got well and the family was reunited.

Another call was from a priest who told Maher of an old couple who was homeless. Maher picked them up. This highlighted another challenge. Maher housing is either all men or all women. Therefore, this couple had to separate and Sister Lucy could see it was so hard on them. Even though the housing was nearby, they could not just be together and hold hands.

Sister Lucy made a plan for housing for couples. There was a new Home being built in Pune in memory of a U.S. devoted supporter via donations by friends and family. Lucy had the architectural plans altered to create a smaller home for women and then add some rooms for couples.

Sister Lucy noticed that even with medicines and hospital care, people recovering from COVID at home were unable to be isolated. (Most homes are only one or two rooms.) Inevitably most if not all of the family got COVID, and it also spread through that village. Maher had been able to stop any spread in Maher homes with immediate quarantine of anyone who became sick. Sister Lucy required that every Maher center have a quarantine space. These spaces were opened for village people recovering from COVID so they could isolate themselves. Maher provided nearly 141 people with free quarantine service and care, such as meals, clothes washing, etc. But these spaces were not enough for all the people in need.

Sister Lucy also saw the need to separate healthy children and adults (especially the elderly) from sick family members. Maher's Bakori Center was quite isolated from other residences and people, so Maher shifted the 50 plus residents and staff from Bakori Center to other area centers, leaving this entire facility empty.

There Maher provided temporary free shelter for children and adults while their parents and family members were recovering from COVID to prevent them from also becoming ill. In this way Maher provided temporary shelter to 168 children and 254 adults in their Bakori temporary shelter home. Maher social workers and staff supported these people.

Additionally masks, soap and hand sanitizers were made widely available. Together, these measures helped slow the spread of COVID.

Summary of Maher's COVID free community programs

- Humanity's Kitchen at Vadhu (more than 30,000 hot meals were served here, though other centers served an additional 12,000 hot meals)

- Grocery kits (over 100,000 distributed over seven states)

- Awareness Programs and personal hygiene education to prevent COVID spread

- 43,000 cloth masks made and distributed

- Hand sanitizers were made and distributed, as well as soap and towels

- 350 Tarpaulin Kits distributed to the poor to cover huts as rainy season set in

- Short-term shelters for children, women, and men: 622 children and 400 adults

- Quarantine Centers in all Maher Ashram homes available to community members (141 people cared for)

- Ambulance services for COVID patients to access medical care: 485 COVID patients transported

- Free nutrition programs in surrounding slums, reaching 615 families: Maher provided eggs, vegetables and vitamins to boost the immune system.

- Counseling services to more than 240 people suffering loss, anxiety from COVD and lockdown via mobile phone; many more were counseled in-person.

- Bakori House converted to family quarantine shelters

During this time, regular operations continued. Maher took new admissions of 221 women, 89 men, 116 children and 14 newborn babies. Maher held 58 skills trainings during COVID lockdown, for 857 participants.

While most of these services were concentrated in Pune District, other sites did what they could. Most centers offered food kits, masks and awareness programs at least.

DAILY LIFE FOR MAHER RESIDENTS DURING LOCKDOWN

Hygiene, masks, home schooling, and lots of activities

Almost no one at any of the Maher Homes got sick; those who did were quarantined immediately. This author finds this miraculous given the great numbers of people living, eating and sleeping in very close quarters. For example, all the children sleep in rows of bedrolls on the floor, side by side. These are then rolled up each morning and the sleeping space becomes the primary living space, where meals are served and home schooling accomplished. There is simply not the space for "social distancing" as was practiced in the West.

Due to the pandemic lockdown, schools were closed for one year. Maher immediately began homeschooling all the children. Staff taught them their lessons, created projects, and organized and supervised activities. The college-going young people's classes were continued online so they were available to help with the younger children as well. Fortunately, most Maher sites now have stable internet.

Given that all the schools had cancelled exams, Maher conducted exams through homeschooling and the children were happy to "keep up and keep learning". At the end of the year, a report card with final results was given to each child. The children who ranked first, second and third were given awards by Sister Lucy.

Dance and music lessons (tabla and singing) and taekwondo classes continued. These enriching activities are core programs at Maher. The activities support health and well-being as young people deal with difficulties and traumas, both from their lives before Maher and from the additional stresses of lockdown. These classes were taught by the college-going young people and graduates of Maher working on site, since the regular teachers could not travel. (Some of Maher's young people have won competition awards in these activities, and some even teach for a living outside Maher.)

Children sitting for homeschooling and exams

Dance class

Tabla class

Yoga, Pranayama and other exercises also continued to keep everyone healthy and fit. Maher regularly promotes the benefits of exercise and diet to keep healthy. For a special program, the Tata Group organized an on-line Zumba dance class for a group of Maher women.

It was an incredible challenge to keep hundreds of children occupied indoors or confined to small outdoor courtyards, keep them from falling behind in their schooling, and keep them from getting into too much mischief. Staff were creative in planning and organizing activities and outings for the children. Sister Lucy appreciated the teachers' efforts throughout the year and presented them with small gifts when the school year ended.

The children of course grew bored during the pandemic, nearly a year kept to one small place. To break the monotony, all the children of Pune were taken for a one-day field trip to Kendur, about 30 kilometers away. During these trips a lot of fun games were organized and food was provided in the fields. Everyone enjoyed the food and scenery. The children were so happy and excited.

During the lockdown, the girls of Sadabahar and Premsagar, the only two Maher Homes inside the city of Pune, were confined to the Home for safety. They were sent to Kendur for an extended stay to get a chance to run and play in the countryside. They were also taken out for field trips. Various games were organized for them.

Similarly, children from Maher's Satara home were taken to Janaimala where they were involved in playing various games and later given a gift. They thoroughly enjoyed their outing.

Field Trip

During the pandemic all of the housemothers took special care of the children without taking a day off. Maher held a gathering for all the area housemothers to express deep gratitude for their dedication. During the program, they were entertained with various activities. Several housemothers were further recognized with small gifts.

Vaccines came to India and Maher a bit later than in the West. At first, to be vaccinated one had to have a government-issued birth certificate and be able to afford payment. Local Maher supporters were able to get Sister Lucy and key staff vaccinated sooner due to their continual outreach which put them at high risk. But people rescued off the streets do not possess birth certificates, even if they once had one. People born in slums or born to migrant families will have never been issued a birth certificate. Therefore, vaccinating all Maher residents was a challenge. All Maher's housemothers and some of the social workers once sought refuge themselves at Maher. Then they later became staff, so even many of them did not have a birth certificate.

Sister Lucy began writing letters to advocate for vaccines for Maher's people with or without ID cards. She addressed well-established networks with local politicians, writing 35 letters in all. Maher Pune became the first organization in Pune area to be able to vaccinate people who had no ID papers. Maher organized several vaccination camps where medical staff came to Maher centers to administer the vaccinations. It took 20 days for vaccinations to be completed for all Maher's residents and staff in Pune District, which encompasses several centers. Maher staff and residents were finally all vaccinated in June 2021. At other Maher locations, staff and residents were ultimately all vaccinated by the end of the summer 2021. Maher also worked to get vaccines into the slums. She had to both reassure the slum dwellers it was safe and convince medical people to come.

Despite COVID other events continued. For example, in Ratnagiri, Maher organized a health camp, with the help of doctors, for children, women and the aged. In this camp, various tests for blood pressure, diabetes and dental tests were conducted. Everyone's height and weight were taken and they were given medicines according to their illnesses.[21]

During COVID and lockdown, life became more difficult and unpredictable. To help overcome the pandemic and its harmful effects, all the centers of Maher conducted prayers one day every month for doctors, nurses, police, and cleaners

---

[21] Maher regularly organizes such medical camps where doctors and nurses come and Maher residents receive free for health check-ups, plus vision and hearing check-ups, for example. Sometimes they can organize these camps for remote villages as well.

who had greatly contributed to society. Prayers were said also to ensure everyone maintained good health.

Work continues in the villages and beyond

Maher's village development work continued, such as empowering women to become financially secure. A training was organized for the Adivasi women at Thakervasti for making washing powder (for clothes). Mr. Rahim, staff designer of products and clothing for Maher's Production, supplied the required materials. He also guided them on how and where to sell the finished product. Or in Kolkata, the women were given training on how to make products from waste. They made make door mats, paper flowers, woolen dolls, pen stands, and more. The women could later sell these products to support their families. These are just two examples of the many training programs that were organized.

Mr. Rahim making washing powder

Making door mats from waste

SERVING THE PEOPLE IN NATURAL DISASTERS: KOLKATA AND THE "SUPER CYCLONE" OF 2020

Maher was only recently established in Kolkata with two small homes on rent when COVID struck. Quickly Maher Kolkata was busy distributing rations and food kits to families in need, providing counseling services, and more. In addition to serving those in their neighborhood, they went to into several slums, the redlight district, rickshaw stands where people gathered, and more. (Even into 2021, many months 1000 kits were distributed each month!)

Soon after the onset of COVID, Kolkata was badly affected by a "Super Cyclone" in the Bay of Bengal. This was the fourth in five years, and one of the strongest storms ever to land here. Many of Kolkata's roads were flooded and millions were without power. COVID restrictions hindered emergency and relief efforts. Social-distancing measures made mass

153

evacuations more difficult, with shelters unable to be used to full capacity. Coastal areas were especially hard hit, including islands. Maher's team was one of the first on the scene to support these areas.

Suprabha told this story:

We (volunteers and Maher staff) went to flood-affected area Sunderbans [mangrove area] with a boatload full of food and supplies. [see photo below] We didn't expect the crowd to be so much! Even with all we brought it was not enough. At the end of distribution one very old lady came. She was so hungry. All we had left was a packet of biscuits. When I saw the way this woman jumped into the flooded muddy water in order to get that biscuit packet, then I understood what was the pain of hunger.

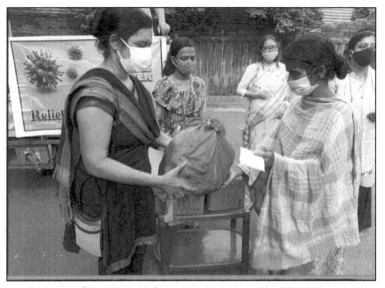

Suprabha (left) passing out grocery kits.

Staff, with help from residents, made grocery ration kits in the morning. Then they loaded these into the Maher jeep and drove several hours (given detours) to get to the people most in need at the coast. Staff drove home late at night and repeated this the next day. And the next. This author spoke to Suprabha late one night, near midnight for her, as they drove home from one such day. She and her staff were still smiling despite how totally exhausted they must have been.

Suprabha also took the initiative to reach out and network with other NGO's. Together they helped nearly 5,086 more families in the Sunderbans (mangrove area) and Digha in West Bengal who had nothing to eat due to the heavy rains and flooding.

155

A headline in a Maher Newsletter noted "Maher Kolkata relief work team serves with love and care to make happiness on every face."

Interfaith: Spreading the Message

In 2017, Maher inaugurated the Interfaith Association for Service to Humanity and Nature. Mangesh Pol was selected to coordinate this new initiative. In this era of heightened inter-religious strife, the goal was to further spread Maher's core value of Interfaith, respecting all faiths, and finding common ground.

Each year Maher holds rallies and events, live and on-line, to embrace the essence of all religions. People come together to honor the values that unite us. Representatives from diverse faiths grace each occasion, standing in solidarity for the service of humanity.

Events include prayers and meditations, "for our souls, our loved ones, our family, friends, Bharatmata, and the entire world, aspiring to fulfill the purpose of humanity."

At Maher it is said "Love is my religion."

From 2024 Interfaith Gathering, which began with a short march to the presentation grounds. The white hats (donated) all say "Peace" and "Love is my Religion."

7: CLOSING THOUGHTS AND LOOKING TOWARD THE FUTURE

As I look toward the future of Maher and my role in supporting this inspiring work, I have two main take-aways.

One is the absolute truth that shelter homes will never be enough to meet the needs of people faced with poverty, violence and despair and how quickly Sister Lucy realized this. She worked to get to the roots of *why* people were seeking shelter. She began focusing on improving the lives of people and families out in the villages.

When people have regular work, a home that provides shelter even in rain and cold, reliable healthy food, then they can send their children to school, care for their families and life is much safer and satisfying. Men and women with employable skills have more self-confidence and better self-worth. Violence and alcoholism decrease. As the next generation gets a good education, they can dream and even achieve those dreams if they work hard. As tolerance for differences (caste, gender, religion especially) grows, villages are more harmonious.

This is a deep truth in our world, and something many in the U.S. are resistant to learning. Maher's Patchwork Quilt of Services can be applied anywhere to improve local lives. Some of these are so simple that any of us can learn from Maher and follow their example. Also, Maher administers all these programs, so social workers can draw from the pool of services to meet families' needs.

From my first visit to Maher in 2010, I have been fascinated by their work in the villages, tribal areas, slums and with other disadvantaged groups such as the beggars' colony you read about in Chapter Two. I saw all these types of communities during my first trip, as well as on subsequent trips. At first, I was skeptical that all the village work really had long-term results but what I have witnessed has made me a big believer. I have wanted to write about Maher's amazing and life-changing work in these communities.

The second take-away is awe at what Maher accomplishes on a relative shoestring of an annual budget and how the full story is not well told.

When Sister Lucy asked a group of us in the U.S. to form a new 501c3 (tax-exempt) organization to collectively support Maher's work with U.S. supporters, and for me to chair it, I accepted. It is hard to say no to Sister Lucy and I care passionately about seeing the work of Maher continue to grow. My increasing knowledge of the impact of Maher on villages, slums and other groups beyond the Maher shelter homes was a big factor in my acceptance.

This book was in process, but therefore went on a back burner while I worked with my colleagues here to get US Giving to Maher founded, IRS approval, and systems established. We are now full steam ahead and this book is getting completed at last.

The new US Giving to Maher board, in communicating with Sister Lucy, realized that a big part of Maher's story was not being shared with donors. We had just reviewed Maher's 2022 financial summary with Sister Lucy. Their entire year's expenditures were just under the equivalency of one million U.S. dollars! If you look at only 65 shelter homes and the care given to each resident, not bad. However, when you consider

159

the, literally, thousands of families and individuals in villages whose lives are changed, these results are astonishing!

In 2021 and 2022 Maher continued all its regular work, plus managed the amazing COVID response and cyclone/flood responses in 2021, plus opened three new centers. Yet their annual budgets (translated to USD) were under one million USD in both years!

Newsletters, ZOOM calls and social media are full of the many heart-warming stories and photos of the residents of Maher shelter homes, and regular recounting of the numbers of residents. The number most often reported for development work in the villages is the number of self-help groups, though their stories are rarely shared. Numbers of kindergartens opened, celebrations held, trainings held, and the like are reported to a handful of us on ZOOM calls, but even here, the impacts of these events on real people's lives could be better shared.

Maher tracks and leverages every rupee and euro and dollar it receives for this incredible impact in terms of lives safe-guarded, families restored, villages uplifted, marginalized people supported into a life of security, children attending school – all that you read here and more. In just one generation these communities are significantly better off, with possibilities for their children once unimaginable to their parents. The before and after descriptions of village life in Thakarvasti are notable and yet not unusual for Maher's work in villages.

For example: recall the Patchwork Quilt of Services most of which focus beyond shelter homes and the numbers Maher generally publishes. All the work with Thakarvasti, the slums, the beggars' colony: mostly this work does not reflect in routinely reported figures. The literacy work, teaching villagers their rights and getting government roads and official recognition, the bore wells, skills training: these things that have radically changed life for the whole village for generations: these success stories do not get widely reported and are mostly unknown.

Perhaps this is in part that change happens slowly. How do you report six months of meetings to build the understanding and trust, to even start the work in a village? Or a couple of years in literacy classes and SHG start-up work prior to results? There was no foundation for any of this work; Maher had to create everything from nothing. I hope this volume is one step in getting this story out to the world.

Finally, I need to again acknowledge the incredible staff of Maher. This volume introduced a few, but more of their stories also could be told, especially those who have been with Maher for 15, 20, even 25 years. They truly live their work. Their children and spouses become part of Maher, even though they live at home. Their families also carry the vision and mission. Currently, some of the professional staff roles are being filled by young people who themselves came to Maher as children, grew up there, went to college and universities, and are now back at Maher, as social workers, office staff, and Board of Trustees members. It is fitting that the future of Maher is looking to its children as they have grown into remarkable young adults!

These young people who grew up and came of age at Maher are living examples of Maher's vision. Whether they work in companies in India, returned to work at Maher as staff, or are raising their own children, they are living the Maher values in daily life. They in turn demonstrate new ways of imagining India's possible future, where all her people may "walk together in dignity towards wholeness."

ACKNOWLEDGEMENTS

First, it is such an honor and a privilege to be connected to Maher and Sister Lucy, the staff, and the residents. I have developed precious friendships over the years with my Maher family. I am in awe of the skill and heartfelt dedication of Sister Lucy and her staff. Witnessing the work of Maher, feeling the palpable love and joy throughout Maher heals and strengthens my own heart. Maher's example helps me "see how it is," and then "do the needful."

No book gets completed without a lot of help. Many of the people of Maher gave me their time, their stories and their skills to help bring to life both this book and the previous one, Rising to New Life: Stories from Maher. Sister Lucy and Hira sat with me many times to explain things, told me Maher history, and took me to experience most of the places in these books. Many told me their stories of their lives before and after Maher. Others have been patient and generous in answering follow-up questions for details via WhatsApp and email. Some of you are: Mathew, Sabita and Jenny, in the office; Maya, a social worker; Mangesh, a Maher grad, now staff. Amol, also a Maher graduate, now staff and in charge of photography and computers, designed the map graphic and the Patchwork Quilt graphic for me to use. Chaya Pamula from US even did a last-minute interview for me, as well as data collection, on her trip to India and Maher a few weeks before going to print!

Finally I wish to thank some early readers of these works who helped me structure the masses of stories and information into two separate books, as well as helped with early editing: Patricia Freeman, Deborah Heller and Ann

Sanders. My mother, Linda Cunningham, read and commented on every version of every chapter. And, finally, my wonderful editor/layout design Tom Holbrook of RiverRun Bookstore without whom this would still be a Word file!

Thank you all.

I offer this book in love and tribute to Maher,
her people, her works.

May all who read it be also uplifted.

APPENDIX 1: MAP OF INDIA

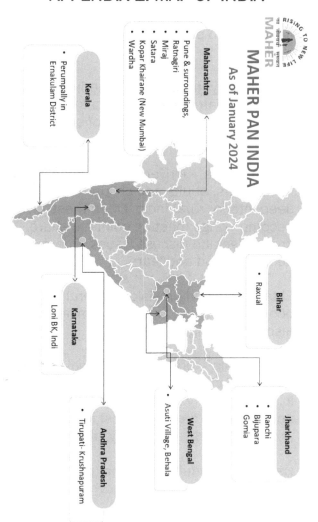

MAHER PAN INDIA
As of January 2024

Maharashtra
- Pune & surroundings,
- Ratnagiri
- Miraj
- Satara
- Kopar Khairane (New Mumbai)
- Wardha

Kerala
- Perumpally in Ernakulam District

Karnataka
- Loni BK, Indi

Andhra Pradesh
- Tirupati- Krushnapuram

West Bengal
- Asuti Village; Behala

Jharkhand
- Ranchi
- Bijupara
- Gomia

Bihar
- Raxual

APPENDIX 2: PATCHWORK QUILT OF SERVICES

1. Aadhar – job placement for village men, women, youth.

2. Adiwasi Kalyan Kendra – ushering in new life for tribals (welfare, advice, services) All the elements of Patchwork Quilt of services, as with Thakarvasti and in Jharkhand.

3. Dnyan Ganga – ("river of knowledge") libraries for villagers, adults and children, especially in deep interior rural India. Often these also become village meeting points to share knowledge and discuss issues. Goal is to inspire people to read and learn.

4. Ekta – free food provisions (monthly rations) for poor families (aim - keeping families together), also counseling as needed

5. Gamatshala – bringing the school to children's doorstep: clean, clothe and feed children, bring in medical professionals ,treat malnourishment and sickness, create interest in schooling. (examples: Beggars' Colony, slums)

6. Kalasagar – adult education (open school to earn high school equivalency)

7. Lokmangala – emergency outreach - immediate support in crisis, for communities and families,

includes grocery kits, tarps, blankets – whatever is needed.

8. Parishram training & production center – for women: tailoring, cards, candles, and other crafts both as soothing activities for easing trauma and earning small sums; but also includes para-social worker and kindergarten teacher certification, plus beautician and tailoring vocational trainings. Craft works are in all Maher centers; crafts and vocational trainings are both offered at Maher centers and taken out to villages and interiors of India.

9. Pragati – awareness and outreach programs (street plays, programs and more)

10. Premalaya – daycare centers (migrant workers, slums, brick kiln workers, tribal areas)

11. Swavalamban – self-help groups

12. Swachata – ("cleanliness") vermiculture pits (compost) in villages and on Maher sites, also indoor toilets, hygienic well maintenance, proper garbage disposal, biogas, solar hot water and more

13. Tantragyan – technical training (computers, cooking, tailoring etc.) Teachers sent to the villages; closely coordinated with Parishram.

14. Ushalaya – kindergartens in remote places while parents work

15. Vidyadhan – support for higher education

16. Vidyalaya – tutoring for underprivileged rural and slum children (usually also includes food)

Additional programs included in Maher's list include the Shelter Homes for women, children, men, elderly women, elderly men, unwed mothers, and Vatsalydham for souls needing additional medical and psychiatric help.

LIST OF PROJECTS

AADHAR	PRISHRAM	USHALAYA	VIDHYALAYA
Job Placement for village youth and Maher youth	Skill Training Unit for village women and young girls including Maher beneficiaries	Kindergartens in villages	Coaching- Computer Classes-Tuition Classes
PREMALAYA	**EKTA**	**SWAVALAMBAN**	**VIDHYADHAN**
Crèche cum Day care center for village children	Providing free provisions to poor families	Self-Help Groups - SHGs	Higher education and professional training for outstation Maher children
KALASAGAR	**SWACHATA**	**PRAGATI**	**DNYANGANGA**
Open school for drop-outs	Construction of lavatories, vermin-culture pits, bio-gas chambers, rain water harvesting, nature conservation in the villages	Rural Outreach & Awareness Programs	Libraries in the villages
ADIVASI KALYAN	**TANTRAGYAN**	**LOKAMANGALA**	**GAMMATSHALA**
KENDRA Awareness and welfare programs for tribal	Center for Vocational Training/ Technical Training for youth	Community Welfare Programs	Play school for children of migrant workers/ daily wage laborer

2

APPENDIX 3: RELIGIOUS SYMBOLS

Om: According to many *Hindu* mystics and philosophers, God is beyond human words and forms. Silence in the presence of the Absolute is considered better than speaking. The uttering and recitation of Om is a stepping-stone to silence. Therefore, a Hindu often begins and ends his prayer by using the mystic monosyllable Om, which stands for the symbolic representation of the Supreme Being in Hinduism.

Dharmachakra: Gautama *Buddha*, after his enlightenment, became the great teacher who set in motion the wheel of dharma. The symbol of a many-spoked wheel with a dot in the center signifies the soul's ultimate liberation from the cycle of birth and rebirth. The wheel may also symbolize a constantly changing universe, the impermanence of everything in the world, and that this journey in search of dharma is an on-going process.

Swastika: *Jainism* follows the religious path established by Vardhamana Mahavira. Swastika is a primitive symbol in the form of a cross with equal arms with limb of the same length projecting at right angles from the end of each arm, all in the same direction, and clock-wise. The word swastika is derived from 'swasti' or well-being, luck and consecration.

Note that this Batik is the international version which omits the swastika of Jainism. Even though it looks quite different from the Nazi symbol based on it, it was offensive to many westerners.

Kara: The steel bangle represents *Sikhism* which is the evolved product of three primary elements – the devotional system taught by Guru Nanak, the structure of Punjabi society and the period of Punjabi history from Guru Nanak to the present day. The five emblems of the Khalsa (chosen race of soldier-saints committed to five principles) are Kesa, Kangha, Kacch, Kirpan and Kara.

Crescent: *Islam,* which belongs to Judaic tradition, is against all symbols. However, the Crescent and the star is used widely to designate Islam. Some scholars allege that the Crescent was adopted as a distinctive mark by the Muslims, in consequence of the Hagira, or flight of Muhammed from Mecca to Medina having taken place at the time of the new moon, when it appears in the form of a Crescent. As the crescent moon gives light to the weary traveler on the hot sands of Arabia, Islam also gives solace to the weary people and guides towards Allah, the Supreme God.

Cross: The principal symbol of the *Christian* religion – cross is beyond doubt the widest used of all Christian symbols. For Christians, the cross is a sign of evoking a historical event basic to the history of salvation: the crucifixion and death of Jesus at Calvary. The sign of the cross is made at liturgical functions, over persons and things.

Star of David: Star of David is the symbol of *Judaism.* The six-pointed star is formulated by two equilateral triangles that have the same center and are placed in opposite directions. It is a dynamic and positive symbol of Judaism.

Bow and Arrow: Bow and arrow is one of the oldest and most used weapons with its origins lost in paleolithic times. These weapons were used by hunters, warriors and people in pursuit of archery as a sport. We can reasonably argue that in prehistoric times too, the hunting and food gathering people had the mental ability to conceive ideas, which can be described as *primordial religion.*

Fire: With a history of some three thousand years, *Zoroastrianism* is one of the most ancient among living religions. It takes its name from its founder, Zarathustra. He recommended meditating before the only basic symbol of the religion – fire.

Yin and Yang: *Taoism*, the religion-philosophy founded by Lao Tse, that traces its roots further into antiquity than any other Chinese belief, has for long utilized this symbol of gracefully bisected circles as its basic symbol. The belief is that there are two primary forces constantly at inter-play in the cosmos; one is the passive female principle, Yin (black) and the other active male principle, Yang (white). However, there is no conflict between these complementary forces.

APPENDIX 4: USEFUL LINKS

Maher Ashram official website
https://maherashram.org/ (includes links to donate
from anywhere in the world)

Maher's (maine) Facebook page
https://www.facebook.com/maher.ashram.india

US Giving to Maher (U.S. 501c3 created to support
Maher's work)
https://usgivingtomaher.org/

U.S. Giving to Maher is a 100% volunteer organization.
Donations through this site go directly to Maher, less 1-
2% for fees such as PayPal, website hosting, etc. We
also host periodic ZOOMs with Sister Lucy to learn
about current events and challenges at Maher, ask
questions, and be inspired. Use the "contact us" form
on our website to join us! USGM is Lucy's official
host/organizer when she comes to the U.S.

To donate directly: (this link is also on US Giving to
Maher's website)
https://givebutter.com/USGM

Made in United States
Troutdale, OR
03/18/2024

18545857R00106